Date Due

ANWAR SADAT

RAYMOND
CARROLL

ANWAR SADAT

FRANKLIN WATTS
NEW YORK I LONDON I TORONTO I SYDNEY I 1982
AN IMPACT BIOGRAPHY

A GROLIER COMPANY

Photographs courtesy of
Wide World Photos: p. 4, 34;
United Press International Photo:
pp. 9, 37, 40, 53, 56,
69, 78, 85, 86, 93, 102;
© David Burnett 1981,
Contact Press Images: p. 18.

Library of Congress Cataloging in Publication Data

Carroll, Raymond.
Anwar Sadat.

(An Impact biography)
Bibliography: p.
Includes index.
Summary: Traces the life of the Egyptian leader from
his humble beginnings, through his military career and
years in prison, to his years as president of Egypt and
his outstanding efforts to make peace with Israel.
1. Sadat, Anwar, 1918–1981—Juvenile literature.
2. Egypt—Presidents—Biography
—Juvenile literature. [1. Sadat, Anwar, 1918–1981.
2. Egypt—Presidents] I. Title.
DT107.85.C37 1982 962'.054'0924 [B] [92] 82-8542
ISBN 0-531-04480-7   AACR2

CONTENTS

ANWAR SADAT

AN ACT OF INFAMY

1

"He who cannot change the very fabric of his thought
will never be able to change reality
and will never, therefore, be able to make progress."

ANWAR SADAT

Anwar Sadat was a rare specimen among the political leaders of our time. Unlike may of his contemporaries, he knew that to achieve great things he must dare great things. And he acted on that knowledge: he dared. The son of a minor civil servant, he rose to become president of Egypt; even more important, he became a statesman of vision and audacity, a leader who had the rare capacity to cast aside old patterns of thought when he found them wanting. It is safe to say that Anwar Sadat belonged to that small breed of twentieth century statesmen who altered the landscape of history.

All his life, Sadat flirted with danger. He took desperate chances as a young man, plotting against the Egyptian monarchy and the British colonizers. As president, he made bitter enemies by abruptly changing policies inherited from his predecessor, Gamal Abdel Nasser. He enraged the Soviet Union by ejecting its military personnel and turning to the United States for friendship. He risked greatly when he matched

Egypt against previously invincible Israel in the October War of 1973 and emerged with enough of a victory to make his countrymen proud to be Egyptian again.

Sadat was to take even greater risks than that in a far different cause: peace with Israel. In defiance of most Arab states, he made an historic pilgrimage to Jerusalem, the heart of the enemy camp, thereby starting a process—unfinished as yet—that he hoped would lead to a full and just peace between Arab and Israeli.

If Sadat shattered the myth of Israeli military invincibility, he also demolished another, even more destructive myth in his visit to Jerusalem and later Camp David: the widely-held belief that Arabs and Israelis could face each other only on the battlefield, never over the negotiating table. For his efforts on behalf of peace, Sadat won millions of admirers around the world, and in 1978 the Egyptian leader shared the Nobel Peace Prize with Israeli Prime Minister Menachem Begin. Typically, Sadat gave his share of the $164,000 prize to his native village.

Not everyone admired Sadat. He made many thousands of determined enemies in the Arab world, antagonists who could not forgive him for making peace with Israel. He infuriated Islamic fundamentalists with his liberal, pro-western inclinations. Sadat knew that his life was in constant peril, but he never flinched. "I will not die," he said fatalistically, "one hour before my time."

That time came on October 6, 1981, the anniversary of the Egyptian assault on Israeli forces in the Sinai in 1973, a holiday dear to Sadat's heart. In the reviewing stand across from the pyramid-shaped Tomb of the Unknown Soldier in Cairo, the Egyptian smiled approvingly as units of his country's armed forces passed smartly before him. At about 12:40 P.M., halfway through the parade, six Mirage jet fighters swept low overhead, trailing plumes of smoke across the azure sky.

*Egyptian President Anwar Sadat, moments before
he was struck down by assassins.*

As everyone, including President Sadat, gazed upward at the aerial display, a truck towing an antitank gun braked to a halt directly in front of the reviewing stand.

In moments, three men in military uniforms jumped from the back of the truck and a fourth leaped from the passenger seat. As they raced toward the reviewing stand, spectators at first thought it was part of the show. Sadat himself rose to his feet as if he thought the onrushing quartet was coming to salute him. The unhappy truth dawned, however, when the four opened up with a barrage of grenades and automatic-weapons fire as they charged ahead screaming "Glory for Egypt!" Security guards were taken totally by surprise. As bullets tore into the reviewing stand, spectators screamed and stampeded for the rear exits. But Sadat, typically, refused to cower. "We tried to pull him down, but he stood up in defiance," said Deputy Prime Minister Fuad Mohieddin. "That was his nature. That was the last lesson from Anwar Sadat."

Sadat, an easy target in his military uniform and green presidential sash, was riddled with bullets. As security guards pursued the fleeing assailants, the Egyptian president was rushed by helicopter to Maadi Military Hospital, south of Cairo. With at least five bullets and shrapnel in his body, Sadat bled copiously from the mouth as he reached the hospital. "I knew he was finished," said Hosni Mubarak, Sadat's vice-president and soon-to-be successor. "I saw all the blood. I just couldn't believe it." Nevertheless, a team of doctors worked furiously on the stricken Sadat, while his wife Jihan waited outside the operating room. After more than an hour, a doctor emerged from the operating room and broke the news to Mrs. Sadat. Tears streaming down his face, the doctor recited a line from the Koran: "Only God is immortal."

Mrs. Sadat tried to maintain her composure, but when she reached the hospital door, she broke down and wept. "I expected him to be killed," she said. "But my husband never expected it. He wouldn't wear his bullet-proof vests because he thought it wasn't manly." In addition to Sadat, seven others died in the hail of gunfire at the reviewing stand.

ENEMIES OF PEACE

News of the assassination quickly spread around the world, stunning western Europe, the United States and particularly Israel. In Jerusalem, a shaken Prime Minister Begin refused at first to believe reports of Sadat's death. When he became convinced, the Israeli leader slumped into his library chair, reflecting on the special moments—both political and personal—he had shared with the dead Egyptian president. Once determined foes, the two men had developed close ties in the tough give-and-take of making peace. "It went beyond matters of state," commented an Israeli official. "Begin mourned the death personally." Begin himself declared: "President Sadat was murdered by the enemies of peace. His decision to come to Jerusalem . . . will be remembered as one of the great events of our time."

In Washington, confirmation of Sadat's death plunged the White House and Capitol Hill into profound gloom. When aides informed Ronald Reagan of Sadat's death, the American president, himself the object of an attempted assassination earlier in the year, mumbled over and over: "Good God, Good God." Then Reagan placed American forces in the Middle East on a higher state of readiness—a symbolic gesture of comradeship for Egypt and a warning to those who might try to gain advantage from Sadat's death. Later, President Reagan paid eloquent tribute to the fallen Egyptian. "He stood in defiance of the enemies of peace," said the president. "Let our words of warning to them be clear: in life you feared Anwar Sadat but in death you must fear him more. For the memories of this good and brave man will vanquish you.

The meaning of his life and the cause for which he stood will endure and triumph.''

Of his close personal friend, Anwar Sadat, former Secretary of State Henry Kissinger remarked: ''He transformed our world by an act of will, shaping history according to his own vision, daring to do what all thought impossible. It has been an honor to be one of his contemporaries.'' Other expressions of grief came from capitals in every part of the world. Austrian Chancellor Bruno Kreisky hailed Sadat as ''one of the great personalities of the century.'' François Mitterand, president of France, said, ''the world has lost one of the best among us.''

For most Egyptians, the first indication that something was wrong came when television coverage of the parade was abruptly halted. Not until seven hours after the attack did Mubarak appear on the television screen and grimly tell his countrymen: ''Our leader, loved by millions, hero of war and peace, is dead. God has ordered that Sadat should die on a day which itself is a symbol of him, among soldiers, heroes and people, proudly celebrating the day on which the Arab world regained its dignity.''

Reaction to the news was curiously muted in the streets of Cairo. Eleven years earlier, the city's millions had poured into the streets to express their grief at Nasser's death. This time the streets were quiet. There were no black banners, no portraits of the slain president, no wailing women. One reason was that a state of emergency declared immediately after Sadat's murder forbade public congregations of five or more people. Another, more compelling reason was that most Egyptians assumed from the start that the killers were religious zealots, men who would not hesitate to punish severely anyone publicly mourning the dead Sadat.

In the Arab world, reaction to the brutal murder was predictably mixed. Egypt's allies, Morocco, Oman and the

Sudan, expressed deep shock. Other moderate Arab regimes, such as Saudi Arabia and Jordan, extended polite condolences to the Egyptian people. Sadat's enemies gloated openly at his death. In Libya, flag-waving crowds, egged on by anti-Sadat strongman Muammar Qaddafi, shouted their approval. In Lebanon, Palestinian commandoes, who believed that Sadat had betrayed their cause, danced in the streets as though celebrating a victory. The Palestine Liberation Organization hailed the killing as an "execution" rather than an "assassination," and one PLO leader stated that "we shake the hand that pulled the trigger." To the east, the Ayatollah Khomeini, leader of Iran's fundamentalist revolution, called on Egyptians to "overthrow the dead pharaoh's successors" and establish an Islamic regime.

A DANGEROUS VOID

Sadat's successors moved quickly to assure an orderly transition. Two hours after the fallen leader was pronounced dead at Maadi Military Hospital, the Cabinet met in emergency session and unanimously named Mubarak as prime minister and supreme commander of the armed forces. Next day, the People's Assembly, Egypt's Parliament, nominated Mubarak for the presidency, and a week later the solemn-faced

President Sadat's funeral procession makes its way toward the pyramid-shaped Tomb of the Unknown Soldier where the slain leader was buried.

former air force officer won a resounding "yes" vote from 98.63 percent of the electorate in an uncontested national referendum. Mubarak, who had been carefully groomed by Sadat as his successor, appeared to be firmly in control.

As one of his first acts, Mubarak promised swift justice for the assassins and their accomplices. On November 21, 1981, four accused killers and twenty others charged as their accomplices, were brought to trial before a military court. The leader of the murder team was identified as Lieut. Khaled Ahmed Shawki el-Istambuli: the other three killers were an army sergeant and two civilians posing as soldiers. Chief among the accomplices was Sheikh Omar Abdel Rahman, a blind mufti or expounder of Muslim law, who provided the religious rationale for killing President Sadat. All twenty-four, whose professed goal was a state dominated by Islamic religious law, were convicted and executed five months later in April 1982.

In a display of mourning for Sadat and solidarity with Mubarak, more than eighty nations sent high-ranking representatives to attend Sadat's funeral on October 10. The mourners included kings, prime ministers, foreign ministers and three former American presidents—Richard Nixon, Gerald Ford and Jimmy Carter. Conspicuous by his presence was Israeli Prime Minister Menachem Begin. "It is very sad," Jihan Sadat said to him, "but I am glad he died on his feet and not on his knees."

Through the streets of Cairo, the dignitaries marched solemnly behind a caisson drawing the coffin draped with an Egyptian flag. The caisson rolled on to a white marble crypt guarded by four lancers. As tears coursed down Mrs. Sadat's face, the coffin was lowered into the crypt. Three volleys of rifle fire were sounded. The mourners stared at the epitaph on the tomb of the Arab leader who had made peace with Israel:

In the name of Allah, All Merciful:
Do not consider those killed for the
sake of Allah as dead but alive
with the Almighty.
President Believer Mohammed Anwar Sadat
died on October 6, 1981.
Hero of war and peace. He lived for
the sake of peace and he was martyred
for the sake of his principles.

THE MAKING OF A REBEL

2

Anwar Sadat's beginnings were humble. He was born on Christmas Day, 1918, in Mit Abul-Kum, a drowsy little village in the depths of the Nile delta. One of thirteen children of government clerk Mohammed el-Sadat and his half-Sudanese wife, Anwar—by his own account—had a happy childhood. The family was large and poor: to keep warm at night, Egypt's future president slept atop the oven in the mud-brick house. But the land in the delta was rich, and young Anwar reveled in the simple country life. In his memoirs, *In Search of Identity*, he wrote: "Everything in the village made me ineffably happy: going out to get carrots, not from the green grocer, but from the land itself; slipping an onion in to roast in our oven (while the family baked bread), then taking it out at sundown to eat; our boyish games in the village by moonlight, and the nightly entertainments that took place on a rustic open stage in the heart of the land, with nature all around us and the bare sky above."

His early village experience imbued Sadat with a love for the Egyptian land that he was to retain all his life. The chores he performed on his father's two-and-a-half acre plot gave him such keen pleasure that he reflected in later life: "Trees, seeds, and fruits were all my fellows in existence; we all came out of the land and could never exist without it. The land is firm and tough, so all that belong to it must be equally tough."

Anwar's father was the first person in Mit Abul-Kum to earn a General Certificate of Primary Education, and as a result the villagers referred to him as "the effendi," a man entitled to respect. Anwar himself received his first schooling at the local Koranic Teaching School, where he learned to read and write and commit the Koran to memory. His only tools of learning were a writing tablet and a reed pen; along with his fellow students, he sat on the floor of the classroom. Anwar's Arab dress had a large, deep pocket which he filled with bread crusts and bits of dry cheese in the morning and from which he snatched mouthfuls in the intervals between lessons. A kindly teacher, Sheikh Abdul-Hamid, inspired the young Sadat with a deep love of learning and "the spirit of true faith."

At night, as Anwar stretched out on the oven, his grandmother held him spellbound with special kinds of bedtime stories. They were not traditional tales of romance or battle. Instead, his grandmother told of events in recent history—and particularly of the struggle of some Egyptians to free their land from the British occupation. Anwar's favorite was the ballad of Zahran, which told of a group of villagers who killed a brutal British soldier. When they were caught, some of the Egyptians were whipped; others were hanged. Zahran, their leader, went to the scaffold with head held high. "I realized that there was something wrong with our life," Sadat later wrote. "Even before I saw the British, I learned to hate the aggressors who whipped and killed our people."

The boy's bitterness was understandable. His country had been dominated by the British since 1882, when their troops defeated the Egyptian army and transformed the ancient land into a small piece of a British Empire that stretched to nearly every part of the earth. Britain's stated objective was to bring political stability and financial solvency to a chaotic country; in reality, its often harsh colonial rule assured the ascendancy of the well-to-do classes and ignored the plight of the people at large. In 1922, Britain unilaterally declared Egypt an independent monarchy; but it was independence in name only. British troops remained in the country. Britain still controlled the army, foreign policy, and the economically vital and strategically important Suez Canal. The corrupt, ineffectual kings were under the British thumb; a Parliament existed, but it and the prime ministers the king chose from its ranks did little more than serve the interests of the Egyptian privileged classes and their British overlords. Such was the unhappy Egypt of Sadat's boyhood.

In 1925, Anwar's father was transferred to a post in Cairo, and the family moved into a small house on the outskirts of the capital. It was not far from Al-Qubbah Palace, one of the royal palaces of King Fuad I. The seven-year-old Anwar gave an early sign of the audacity he was to display in later life by stealing apricots from the palace orchard. In those days, anyone caught stealing anything from the king would have been dealt with severely.

The elder Sadat rose to become a senior clerk, but the family remained abysmally poor. They could not afford bread from a store, so they baked their own, just as they had in the village. At school, Anwar became aware for the first time of class differences among the students. Some of them came to school in limousines, bought chocolates in the school canteen and wore beautiful new clothes. Sadat had only enough allowance money to buy a cup of milky tea at school; he owned one threadbare suit which he wore every school day. But he later said he did not envy his wealthier classmates. His early village life, with its "fraternity, co-operation and love," gave him a deep sense of self-confidence. As he wrote in his memoirs: "It deepened my sense of inner superiority, a feeling which has never left me and which, I came to realize, is an inner power independent of all material resources."

In secondary school, Sadat's feelings of patriotism intensified. He hated the red-faced British constable who patrolled his neighborhood on a motorcycle. He took part in schoolboy demonstrations against the British, often without knowing the issues involved. In 1932, the great Indian nationalist leader Mohandas Gandhi visited Egypt on his way to England. The fourteen-year-old Sadat had read about Gandhi and his struggle against British rule in India. In protest against the importation of British-manufactured western clothes into his country, Gandhi wore only a *dhoti*, or traditional Hindu loincloth. He made the cloth for this garment on his own spinning wheel as an example in self-sufficiency for his countrymen. Impressed, young Sadat began to imitate Gandhi, wearing only a loincloth fashioned out of an apron, trying to weave his own cloth and retiring to the roof for solitary contemplation. He abandoned this Gandhi impersonation only after his father finally convinced him that what he was doing could not possibly benefit Egypt but might very well give him a case of pneumonia.

THE YOUNG OFFICER

As he progressed through secondary school, Sadat became convinced that a military career would be the best way to achieve his deepest desire—the deliverance of Egypt from British rule. And so, upon graduation, he applied for entrance into the Royal Military Academy. Ironically, it was a Briton, one Dr. Fitzpatrick, who was instrumental in getting Sadat admitted to the academy. Sadat's father had worked for Fitzpatrick, the chief medical officer in the Egyptian army, and got him to write a glowing letter on his son's behalf. It apparently worked. Anwar was admitted and went through the military

training that was to enable him to realize his ambition—the ejection of the British and the monarchy from his country. In 1938, Sadat graduated from the academy and was commissioned as a second lieutenant in the Egyptian army.

Stationed in Manqabad, a small town in southern Egypt, Lieutenant Sadat began to hold meetings with fellow officers in his room. The topic of discussion was usually Egypt's condition of subservience, and soon Sadat's room came to be called "The National Assembly." As the circle gradually widened, one of the young officers who occasionally attended was Gamal Abdel Nasser, later to become the leader of Egypt's revolution. At the time, Nasser impressed Sadat as a deeply serious and determined young man whose natural aloofness kept a distance between him and his fellow officers.

In 1939, Sadat, to his great delight, was transferred to the newly-formed Signal Corps and stationed in Maadi, outside Cairo. From that central location, the twenty-one-year-old officer stepped up his political activity, holding meetings in cafes, the officers' mess and at his father's house. Encouraged by German victories and British defeats in 1939–1940, Sadat extended his contacts, approaching for the first time senior officers who could be counted on to support an armed revolution against the British. In this way, Sadat and his associates gradually put together a secret organization of army officers; it came to be called the Free Officers' Organization.

Second lieutenant
Anwar Sadat,
shortly after
his graduation
from the Royal
Military Academy.

Sadat was shifted in 1941 to Marsa Matruh, on the Mediterranean, where he devised a plan for immediate revolution. The British were weak and on the defensive at the time, having suffered stunning defeats in Asia, Europe and North Africa. When the British—doubtful of the allegiance of the Egyptian army—ordered all Egyptian units to withdraw from the Marsa Matruh, Sadat proposed to his fellow officers that all their units assemble near the Mena House Hotel, near the end of the Cairo-Alexandria highway. There they would regroup, march into Cairo and seize power. But Sadat, then twenty-two, was to suffer a grievous disappointment. When he arrived with his troops at the Mena House Hotel, no other Egyptian units were in sight. Sadat waited for hours, but still no other units arrived, and it became clear to him that the officers he had counted on had backed down. Sadat's attempt at an armed insurrection had failed—and the authorities were not even aware that it had taken place! "I took it like a sportsman," he wrote later. "Rather than despair, I redoubled my contacts with all army services."

Late in 1941, Sadat became involved in a curious clandestine scheme to use an Egyptian military plane to fly Gen. Aziz al-Masri, who had been ousted as Chief of Staff of the Army because of his anti-British views, out of the country. The plan, conceived by the Germans, envisaged the flight of al-Masri to Iraq, where he was to assume an active role in an anti-British uprising. Some of Sadat's friends seized an Egyptian plane and took off with al-Masri aboard, but the plane ran out of fuel soon after takeoff and crash-landed in a tree. The incident was investigated by the authorities, and Sadat, then a captain, was arrested and interrogated. But the prosecuting attorney could not find any incriminating evidence against him, so Sadat was released and returned to his post. Even though he was implicated in the al-Masri incident and certainly intended to pursue his anti-British activities, Sadat could not help but be impressed by the British-inspired legal system that led to his release. "That shows," he thought on the way back to his desert post, "the advantages of the rule of law."

THE GERMAN CONNECTION

Feelings against the British ran high at the time. Anything that would weaken the British position was of prime importance to Sadat, and that view was shared by a majority of Egyptians. As German General Rommel and his Afrika Corps swept the British before them and took the Egyptian town of El Alamein, just sixty-five miles from Alexandria, the whole country seemed open to German conquest. In Cairo, crowds of Egyptians demonstrated in the streets, chanting "Advance, Rommel! Advance Rommel!" The demonstrators certainly were not supporters of the Nazi cause; they simply saw British defeat as the only way to gain independence for Egypt.

Sadat saw it the same way, but he had no intention of having a British defeat lead to domination by another foreign power. At the time, rumor had it that Egypt, in the event of a German victory, would be handed over to Italy. It was also said that Italian dictator Benito Mussolini had already chosen a white horse on which he would ride into Cairo, just as the Romans had done in ancient times. Sadat and his fellow officers agreed that something had to be done to prevent Rommel from seizing all of Egypt. The Free Officers' Organization therefore drafted a "treaty," under which it offered to recruit an entire army to fight against the British and also provide Rommel with photographs showing the positions and defenses of British forces in Egypt. In return, a victorious Germany would grant Egypt total independence and not place it under Italian or German domination.

Sadat was determined to bring the proposal to Rommel's attention, and so one of the Free Officers, Ahmed Saudi Hussein, was sent off in an Egyptian air force plane, bound for El Alamein. It was another ill-fated plan. The plane was a British-made "Gladiator," and so the Germans naturally shot it down as it approached their positions. Ahmed Saudi was killed and the proposal never reached General Rommel. Fortunately for Sadat, the aircraft incident was not traced to the Free Officers' Organization or to him.

Still determined to present the proposition to Rommel, Sadat made contact with two German agents in Cairo. Nothing came of it, as the two, known to Sadat as Eppler and Sandy, spent much of their time drinking and admiring the dancers at the Kit-Kat nightclub. They had huge amounts of money and spent it freely, inevitably coming to the attention of British intelligence. Before long, the bumbling Eppler and Sandy were arrested and interrogated; the two soon admitted that they were German spies and went on to implicate Sadat. As a result, a swarm of British and Egyptian detectives and intelligence agents descended on the young captain's house. Somehow his hidden cache of homemade arms and a high-powered radio transmitter he had obtained from the Germans went undetected. Sadat nevertheless was arrested and taken into detention. He stubbornly denied any guilt, insisting that he thought the two Germans were British officers. He was not believed, and finally Sadat was stripped of his rank and taken off to the Aliens' Jail in Cairo.

After a short spell in the Aliens' Jail, a prison reserved for cases connected with the war, Sadat was moved along to a series of detention centers over the next two years. It was not, by any means, wasted time. Sadat read widely in Arabic and English; he studied German. And he spent hour after hour in self-examination, perceiving personal traits he had never suspected before. Beyond the liberation of Egypt, he discovered, there was little he wanted for himself, not fame, not power, not wealth. All he needed to be happy, he thought, was a couple of acres of land to farm and call his own.

By late 1944, it had become quite obvious that the allies, including the British, were going to emerge victorious from

World War II. Something had to be done, Sadat thought; he could not remain in jail indefinitely. In October, Sadat—as part of an escape plan—went on a hunger strike. In accordance with official regulations, he was moved to Qasr al-Ayni Hospital. There he ended his hunger strike and began to recuperate. One day during the crowded lunch hour, he dodged his guard, jumped into a friend's car parked outside and sped out of the hospital grounds. Within minutes, he arrived at a pre-arranged hideout, where he began a year-long period as a fugitive.

During that year, Sadat disguised himself by growing a beard and going by the name of Hadji Muhammad. As he had to earn money to support himself and his family, he worked as a porter for a man who sold supplies to the British army. He then got a job as a laborer on a canal project, and finally was hired to transport marble from a quarry to a site near the Pyramids. The marble was for the construction of a royal "resthouse" for King Farouk, a man he was later to help depose and drive into exile.

ASSASSINATION PLOTS

With the end of World War II, martial law—under which Sadat had been detained—was terminated. This meant that there was no longer any legal basis for his detention. In September 1945, he put an end to hiding and resumed a normal life, returning home and abandoning his disguise. It seems likely that Egyptian and British intelligence kept an eye on Sadat, but that did not deter him. He was as eager as ever to plot the overthrow of the monarchy and British colonial rule. "So, the minute I regained my freedom," he later recalled, "I started to form a secret organization, feeling that personal liberty could hardly be real until my entire homeland had been liberated."

As a first step, Sadat and his co-plotters decided to take

violent measures against Egyptian politicians who cooperated with the British. They staged a grenade attack on Mustafa el-Nahas, head of the Waftists, a party the conspirators considered disloyal to Egypt because it worked within the British-imposed political system. The attack failed when the explosion barely missed el-Nahas' car. Next, they focused their attention on Amin Osman Pasha, an aristocratic politician who strongly supported the British presence in Egypt. Pasha's pro-British statements, Sadat later said, were "tantamount to a self-imposed death sentence." On January 6, 1946, the death sentence was carried out. As Pasha entered the headquarters of his "Revival League" in Cairo, a young member of Sadat's group named Hussein Tewfik called out: "Pasha! Pasha!" When Pasha turned around, Tewfik drew his pistol and shot him dead.

The assassination received widespread attention in the press, and Sadat was convinced that the act of terrorism achieved its objective. It removed a staunch supporter of colonialism, and it seriously damaged the prestige of the British authorities in the eyes of the Egyptian people. The police soon rounded up Tewfik, however, and he named Sadat as a co-conspirator. In the middle of the night, police arrived at Sadat's houe and dragged him off once again to the Aliens' Jail.

Sadat's group of anti-British conspirators was not the only one operating in Egypt at the time, and it may have been one of the smallest. But it had achieved enormous public attention by assassinating a leading pro-British political figure, and so Sadat—as one of the leading members of the ring—was regarded by the Egyptian and British authorities as an important catch. Unlike his earlier stay in Aliens' Jail, this time he was placed in solitary confinement. Despite intensive questioning, however, he refused to admit any guilt in the Pasha killing. In a calculated attempt to confuse matters, Sadat accused the prison guards of torturing him. The accusation was false, but it succeeded in disturbing the authorities, and so the prosecuting attorney finally sent the troublesome Sadat to the far more forbidding Cairo Central Prison. His first impressions of the place remained vividly in his mind many years later:

"It was four o'clock in the afternoon when I found myself inside Cell 54. I looked around. Cairo Central Prison was completely different from the Aliens' Jail. In the first place, there was no bed, no small table, no chair and no simple lamp. It was completely bare—apart from the palm-fibre mat on the macadamized floor, hardly big enough for a man to sleep on, and an unbelievably dirty blanket. You can't imagine how filthy that thing was. In the winter water oozed from the cell walls day and night, and in the summer huge armies of bugs marched up and down . . . . I lived for a whole eighteen months in that hole, unable to read or write or listen to the radio. I was denied everything, even a single lamp."

Sadat's intense feelings about conditions in the prison were to surface three decades later when he was president of Egypt. To start the destruction of an old prison, Sadat was supposed to take a pickax and deliver a ceremonial blow to the wall. With his first blow, the rotten wall started to crumble, releasing hordes of cockroaches. Disgusted, Sadat kept hitting at the wall, as though he could demolish it himself. Aides tried to get him to stop, but he kept smashing away at the wall. As he wrote in his memoirs, "I was dominated by the feeling that such prisons should be removed and replaced by others fit for human beings."

SELF-EXAMINATION

In the stark isolation of Cell 54, Sadat had plenty of time for self-examination. He had no links with the outside world; and so he was forced to turn inward. One of the most painful areas of self-examination was his marriage. In typical country fashion, he had married early, by family arrangement, with one of his relatives. But for some time, it had become clear to Sadat that he and his wife had very little in common. He felt certain that he was destined to play a role as a revolutionary leader and that his wife would never be happy married to a man with such a dangerous and unpredictable calling. He felt like a traitor for even considering a break with his wife. But finally, he made a decision. First, he stopped his wife from visiting him in prison. Later, after his release, he told her that it would be impossible for the two of them to stay together. A divorce followed soon after.

After a while, the prison authorities allowed Sadat to have books, magazines and newspapers, which he read voraciously. When an idea, a poem or anything written, either by an eastern or western author, appealed to him, he copied it out in his prison notebook. The wide-ranging reading broadened his knowledge and helped him to know himself better. One of the things the solitary prisoner thought about most deeply was man's relationship with God, and Sadat came to the conclusion that it should not be based on fear, or on the expectation of reward, but on mutual love. This mutual love between man and God, he reflected, would establish a bond that would always bring peace of mind, no matter how difficult the circumstances.

By Sadat's own account, his deepening love of God led to profound changes in his view of the world. He found that he could no longer bring himself to hate anybody, even those who hated him. He decided that, by nature, he was committed to love. As he later wrote: "To love means to give, and to give means to build, while to hate is to destroy." Immersed in such thoughts, Sadat found his last months in Cairo Central Prison an extremely happy period.

When Sadat's case was finally brought to trial, it proved to be a long, drawn-out process, lasting from January to August 1948. He was still in jail when the first Arab-Israeli war broke out in May 1948. To Sadat, it was agonizing to sit in prison while Israeli aircraft raided Cairo. He desperately wanted to be out fighting, but he was helpless and could do nothing to aid the Arab cause.

Sadat knew that, if he were found guilty of complicity in Pasha's assassination, he would face a death sentence or hard labor for life. But as the trial dragged on, month after month, Sadat and his co-defendants got plenty of attention in the press. Egyptian public opinion backed them strongly, and supporters hired the best lawyers in Egypt to defend them. Meanwhile, Tewfik—the actual assassin who had turned state's evidence—kept changing his story and confusing the prosecution. Tewfik finally escaped before the trial came to a close.

In early August, the day of sentencing arrived. Sadat put on an old white jacket and gray trousers, all the clothes he owned, and was taken to court. When he heard that Tewfik, number one on the list of defendants, was sentenced *in absentia* to a relatively light ten years in prison, Sadat felt confident that he would be acquitted. He was right. After a few agonizing moments, the judge pronounced Anwar Sadat not guilty. Once again, after two and a half years in prison, he was a free man.

REVOLUTION
AND AFTER

3

For months after his acquittal, Sadat floundered, not knowing which way to turn. He worked as a rewrite man at a publishing house and joined in a number of business ventures with an old friend, Hassan Izzat. For a time the arrangement worked, and Sadat made enough money to propose marriage to a beautiful young woman he had met at Hassan Izzat's home. Her name was Jihan Safwat and she was half-Egyptian, half-British. She accepted, in the Egyptian tradition, only after her father gave his blessing and accepted the proposal. The two were married on May 29, 1949.

Before long, Sadat had a falling out with his partner. Hassan Izzat took to haggling over money, and Sadat—not a businessman at heart—was deeply offended. In a rage, he told off Hassan Izzat and put an end to their relationship. The break made things clear to Sadat. The only way to accomplish his real mission in life, revolution against the corrupt monarchy and the hated British, was to go back to the army.

Legally, there was nothing to prevent Sadat's return to the military. Some of the top brass regarded Sadat as a troublemaker and opposed his return. But in January 1950, after getting a well-placed friend to pull some strings, Sadat was reinstated in the army as a captain, the same rank he held when he was dismissed. Gamal Nasser, then a lieutenant colonel, was among the first to welcome him back to the ranks; he quickly brought Sadat up to date on the Free Officers' Organization. During Sadat's years in prison, Nasser had taken over leadership of the organization, which had become tremendously powerful in all branches of the military. How much influence the underground network had gained was quickly made clear to Sadat when Nasser advised him to ask for a promotion; to his surprise, he was promptly promoted to major.

In Sadat's absence, Nasser had introduced into the Free Officers' Organization a cell system modeled after Marxist conspiratorial groups. The organization permeated the military establishment, but the membership in each cell was unknown outside the cell itself and members of a cell did not know the identity of the overall leadership. The leadership itself was a shadowy group of radical nationalists, democratic socialists and pro-Moscow Marxists, with Nasser at its center. In 1951, however, Nasser decided that the time had come for the organization to have a more formal command structure. He therefore established a "Constituent Council" as the highest body in the organization. Some of its members were old friends of his like Abdel Hakim Amer; some were officers he knew personally from the first Arab-Israeli war; others were original leaders of the organization, including Sadat.

Sadat, though not in Nasser's immediate circle at first, quickly became an influential member of the council. As a revolutionary with impeccable credentials, he was able to dissuade Nasser from embarking on a large-scale campaign of political assassination. Sadat argued that the effort required for such an operation should be made in behalf of the revolution itself. "Let us advance to our objective directly," he said, "let us have our revolution." Nasser became convinced that Sadat was right; the course of terrorism, one which Sadat had already tried, was dropped from the officers' revolutionary agenda.

THE REVOLT

In late 1951 and early 1952, an apparently spontaneous tide of anti-monarchy, anti-British feeling swept over Egypt, giving Nasser, Sadat and their fellow plotters hope that full-scale revolution might not be just a pipe dream. In early January 1952, their Constituent Council met and targeted November 1955 as the date for the uprising. But a few days after the meeting, violent riots—anti-monarchy and anti-British in tone—erupted in Cairo. The explosion, generally attributed to a long-repressed bitterness among the Egyptian people caused by poverty and subjugation, seemed to take anti-government groups of all political views by surprise. With anger and discontent—the very smell of revolution—in the air, Sadat and the other council members decided to reassess their revolutionary timetable. Through a contact he had in the royal palace, Sadat was able to learn that King Farouk—badly shaken by the riots—was convinced that he could not survive for long on the throne. In fact, he had already started to smuggle his gold out of the country and into Swiss banks. When Sadat reported this to the council, it decided to speed up its planning and set the revolution for November 1952. Later, however, a journalist told Nasser that the king was considering the appointment of a tough new war minister who was well-informed about the Free Officers' Organization and was determined to destroy it. It was clear that the plotters had to move fast. The timetable was again speeded up. The revolution would take place in July.

On July 21, Sadat, then stationed at Al-Arish, received an urgent message from Nasser: meet him in Cairo the following day; the revolution would take place betweeen the 22nd and the 25th. Sadat arrived in Cairo the next day, but Nasser was not, as he usually was, at the train station to meet him. Thinking that he had arrived too soon, Sadat took his wife Jihan to the movies, and when they returned home the porter told him that Nasser had been trying to reach him and had left a message. It said that the operation would begin that night. "My heart leapt," Sadat recalled in his book *Revolt on the Nile*. "I tore off my civilian clothes and threw on my uniform. In five minutes I was at the wheel of my car."

Soon Sadat was at Al-Abbasiah army barracks, where the rebels had already stormed the Army Command Headquarters and arrested the top military officers. At Nasser's direction, Sadat took command of the telephones, contacting rebel leaders in the Sinai, the Western Desert, Alexandria, Al-Qantara East, Al-Arish and Rafa. By three o'clock in the morning, Sadat was able to report that everything was proceeding smoothly on all fronts. The dream to which the thirty-three-year-old Sadat had devoted his entire life—for which he had spent years in prison—was finally coming true.

But so far, only the first step had been taken. Next, Nasser told Sadat to take over the Cairo radio station and broadcast a proclamation announcing the coup. At daybreak on July 23, Sadat made his way to Broadcasting House. After waiting for the daily reading from the Koran to be completed, he jubilantly announced the birth of the revolution. When he left the building, he saw the streets of the metropolis crowded with people as never before. Egyptians of all ages and classes were kissing each other, gathering in clusters and shaking hands. But all the time the people were strangely quiet. They were overjoyed by what they had heard on the radio but they were not totally convinced that the old order was really finished. It was, said Sadat, a "festive silence."

King Farouk, at the time, was in his summer residence in Alexandria, and so on the 26th of July rebel troops moved down from Cairo and laid siege to Ras al-Tin Palace. Sadat, who had been chosen by the Constituent Council to deliver an ultimatum to the king, shocked Farouk's aides when he read it out to them that morning. The ultimatum demanded that the king leave Egypt by six o'clock that evening; if he failed to do

Army tanks lined the streets of Alexandria following the abdication of King Farouk on July 26, 1952.

so, he would suffer the consequences. Within an hour and a half, the king accepted the ultimatum. Sadat immediately got in touch with the captain of the royal yacht *Mahroussa* and asked him to have the boat ready to take the royal family into exile that evening at 6:00. Sadat then ordered the coast artillery not to fire on the yacht as it sailed away and told the air force to execute a flyover salute to the deposed king when the ship left Egyptian waters.

Farouk left Egypt on time, at 6:00 on the evening of July 26, 1952. Nasser had seen him aboard; Sadat stood on the deck of the warship *Ibrahim* in Alexandria harbor, watching the aircraft circle in salute to the king. As Sadat wrote later, "It was a simple gesture, I thought, but sufficiently implied our self-confidence, pride and tolerance—the emanation of the spirit of Egypt down the centuries."

PROBLEMS OF POWER

While the monarchy was being overthrown, Britain—resigned to Farouk's ouster and its own eventual departure from Egypt—did nothing to interfere. British troops remained in their barracks. The Egyptian Parliament and Prime Minister Ali Maher took a low profile. Though Maher had been appointed by Farouk, Nasser—seeing the need for some sort of governmental continuity—convinced him that he must stay on as prime minister at the head of a new cabinet. In another move, Nasser changed the name of the Constituent Council—the ruling body of revolutionary officers—to the Revolutionary Command Council. Nasser was unanimously chosen as its chairman—and therefore the real leader of Egypt.

In the months that followed, Sadat was appalled to see some of his colleagues on the council engage in constant rounds of backbiting and intrigue, each seeking to gain more power. Sadat could not fully restrain his contempt for some of them. They had never known poverty or homelessness or prison, as he had. But in a matter of days, they were vaulted from their army offices to positions of great power in the country. Young and ambitious, they seemed to care more for their own personal advancement than for the success of the revolution.

Slowly, Sadat became aware that he was the object of considerable animosity among his colleagues. At first he was puzzled, then he reflected that they were annoyed at the highly visible role he had played in announcing the revolution to the country and in delivering the ultimatum to King Farouk. In addition, Sadat was the only council member known to the public, in large part because the mass media had given him plenty of attention during the Amin Osman case.

Sadat refused to join his colleagues in a struggle for grander titles and greater power. They, in turn, tried to turn Nasser against him. Nasser was a deeply suspicious man, and he often placed credence in the most unlikely tales brought to him by people trying to gain his approval. Sadat suspected that some of his adversaries on the council had told Nasser that he could not be trusted; moreover, Sadat noticed that Nasser had become cool towards him. Sadat was hurt, but he drew on his experience in Cell 54 of Cairo Central Prison and remembered that his own integrity was a greater thing than any post or title.

In September 1952, the council replaced the figurehead prime minister, Ali Maher, with another figurehead, Major-General Muhammad Naguib. At the same time, some of the old politicians, in connivance with certain army officers, tried to hatch a plot against the revolution. On January 16, 1953, the council abruptly disbanded all the old political parties, placed a number of politicians under temporary detention and court-martialed the officers who conspired with them. In addition, the council assumed all legislative and executive power in the country for a period of three years; it also issued a decree outlawing the Muslim Brotherhood, the fanatical

As a member of President Nasser's Revolutionary
Command Council, Lt. Col. Anwar Sadat signed the
proclamation declaring Egypt a republic.

Islamic secret society intent on taking over the rule of Egypt and imposing a religious tyranny on the country.

In March 1953, Nasser took other decisive actions. With the approval of the council, Egypt was declared a republic and the property of the royal family was confiscated. Naguib was installed as president, while Nasser—the actual leader— gave himself the posts of deputy premier and interior minister. At one stroke, Nasser also promoted his old friend Abdel Hakim Amer from the rank of major to major-general and named him commander in chief of the armed forces. The elevation of Amer to high position was to prove a fateful move for Egypt.

In late 1952 and early 1953, the young revolutionary regime could already point to some accomplishments. The Agrarian Reform Law, which was to change the face of Egypt, had been put into effect. To the dismay of the large land owners and the traditional politicians, the law limited land ownership to a little over 200 acres (80 hectares) and distributed plots of land to poor landless farmers. Sadat was particularly pleased that the millions of dollars derived from the confiscated royal property was put into rural health centers, hospitals and schools. He exulted in the fact that in one year alone as many new schools were built in Egypt as in the previous twenty years. During that same period, the idea of a High Dam on the Nile at Aswan was taken under consideration by the council, and in 1953 work was started on a hydroelectric station at the old Aswan Dam—a station that eventually was to generate the power needed to begin work on the High Dam in the 1960's.

The first years of the revolution also saw momentous changes in Egypt's relations with the world at large. The country badly needed a non-British source of arms, and at first the council approached the United States and offered to buy weapons. The Eisenhower Administration, whose foreign policy was dominated by John Foster Dulles, answered that the United States would supply the weapons free, provided that Egypt signed a mutual security pact with the United States. Other conditions were that American experts had to come along with the weapons and that the arms could never be used against a U.S. ally. Not surprisingly, the council angrily rejected Washington's offer. Egypt did not want free arms; it wanted to buy arms without any strings attached and it was in no mood to join yet another one of the many pacts devised by Secretary of State Dulles to contain the expansionist tendencies of the Soviet Union.

Nasser and the council then turned to Moscow for arms, and Soviet dictator Josef Stalin, who would not sell arms to non-Communist countries, flatly refused. Not until 1955 did the Soviets, then led by Nikita Khrushchev, change their minds, and in September of that year an arms deal was signed between Egypt on one side and Soviet Union and Czechoslovakia on the other. The refusal of the United States to sell arms without strings thus led to close—if not permanent—military ties between Cairo and Moscow.

To the distress of Egypt's revolutionary leaders, British troops remained in the country two years after the revolution. In 1954, however, Nasser embarked on negotiations for their withdrawal; the talks moved along swiftly. The British took the position that they would evacuate the Suez Canal base, their military center, within twenty-four months but would retain some of their stores and about 1,200 civilian experts in Egypt for seven years. After that, the stores and anything else left at the base would belong to Egypt. At this point, Nasser, eager to know the views of the council, called a meeting at the official conference center, the Pyramids Resthouse. Some of the council members quibbled interminably over the smallest points, much to Sadat's annoyance. "What is there to be discussed?" he asked. "The British want to retain some 1,200 non-military experts who would thus be guarded by us, the Egyptians; will such experts frighten us? . . . Only a stu-

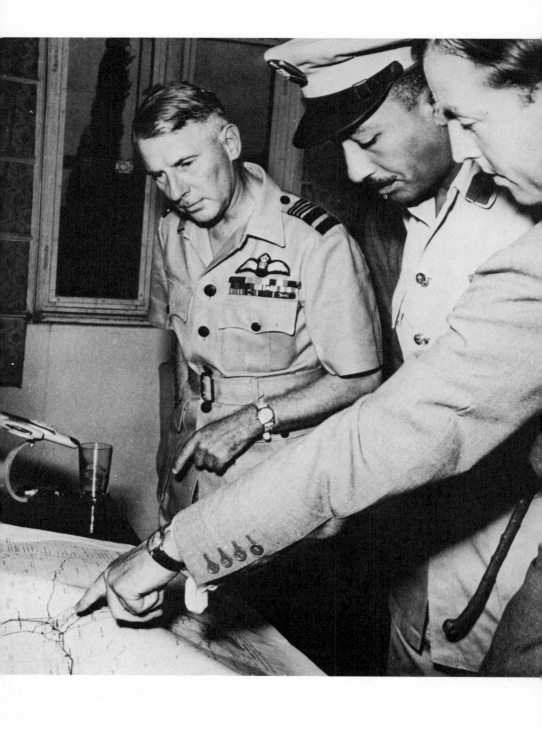

pid politician could reject such a solution to a problem that is over seventy-five years old." Most of the council agreed, and the draft was accepted. The Anglo-Egyptian Evacuation Agreement was signed on October 19, 1954. The last British soldier left Egypt twenty months later; after seventy-five years, the Union Jack was hauled down and the Egyptian flag raised over the military base in the Canal Zone.

Sadat confers with
British officials
at the Suez Canal
base around the time
of the signing of
the Anglo-Egyptian
Evacuation Agreement.

TURNING
POINTS

4

The years from 1953 through 1956 were highly eventful ones for Egypt, for its revolutionary government and for Sadat. Immediately after signing the evacuation treaty with Britain, Nasser decided to reshuffle the government. Naguib was sacked. Nasser took on the post of premier and, of course, remained as chairman of the all-powerful council. Sadat, though reluctant to accept a government post, agreed to serve as minister of state and became one of Nasser's chief troubleshooters in the cabinet.

THE BAGHDAD PACT

The British, as it turned out, may have been resigned to seeing their old domination of large parts of the Middle East come to an end, but they still hoped to retain a large measure of influence in the region. After the signing of the evacuation agreement, British Prime Minister Anthony Eden engineered the creation of the so-called Baghdad Pact. Eden's rationale was that a "vacuum" had arisen in the Middle East as a result of the withdrawal of British power from the region, and that the vacuum had to be filled or the Soviet Union would expand its power in the area. Turkey, Iraq and Pakistan quickly joined the pact, But Egypt was in no mood to adhere to a British-dominated agreement and said so in the clearest terms. Not only did Cairo reject participation in the pact, it actively campaigned against it in the Arab world, calling on the other states to refuse membership.

One of Sadat's positions at the time was as secretary-general of the Islamic Congress, an organization dedicated to strengthening ties among the Arab states, and in that role he did much to frustrate Eden's plans. Flying to Jordan, he was able to persuade that country's King Hussein not to join the pact; in Lebanon, he used President Camille Chamoun's well-known antipathy toward the Turks to convince him that he should stay clear of Eden's arrangement. Sadat also established a new newspaper, *al-Gumhuriah* (The Republic) and assumed the post of editor-in-chief. As such, he wrote many articles attacking the Baghdad Pact, articles which had considerable influence throughout the Arab world.

Egypt's determined opposition to the Baghdad Pact angered both Britain and the United States, who—or so Sadat was convinced at the time—encouraged an Israeli raid on the Egyptian area of Gaza on February 28, 1955. The Israelis maintained that the punishing raid was strictly a reprisal against terrorists operating in the region. Whatever the real reason for the raid might have been, it made the Egyptians realize just how vulnerable they were and how much they needed modern weapons. Nasser kept pressing the Soviet Union, and later that year the first arms deal with the Soviet Union was signed. The deal boosted Egyptian morale, but also lifted the spirits of other small, non-Communist countries and liberation movements, who had learned that Moscow was prepared to supply arms for "anti-imperialist" causes.

In the early 1950's, Nasser became something of a folk hero to many in the Third World. One of his moments of glory came in 1955, at the first Conference of Non-Aligned Countries held at Bandung, Indonesia. The conference established the non-aligned group—countries which, theoretically at least, owed no allegiance either to the Soviet bloc or the West—as a force to be reckoned with in world affairs. At the conference, Nasser became extremely visible to the world at large as he hobnobbed with such international figures as Jawaharlal Nehru of India, Sukarno of Indonesia and Chou En-Lai of China. Nasser's popularity at home was given an enormous boost. Some of the members of the council were irritated by all the publicity Nasser received, and Sadat believed they were jealous of his success. To Sadat, Nasser's prestige was Egypt's prestige and therefore something to be celebrated.

Increasingly, Sadat became disturbed by the conduct of his colleagues on the council, their incessant bickering, their petty hatreds and their jealousies, their constant struggle to expand their power and use it arrogantly. In Sadat's mind, the heads of these supposed revolutionary leaders had been turned by power. Believing that they were "benevolent dictators," they were convinced that they could impose anything they wanted on the people. They went so far as to divide the country into personal "spheres of influence," within which they could turn a profit for themselves and produce rewards for their followers and friends.

In June 1956, Nasser was formally elected president of Egypt in a national plebiscite, and shortly thereafter he dissolved the Revolutionary Command Council. Sadat was delighted. He felt that too many of its members were power-mad bullies. "Fear reigned everywhere," Sadat later wrote, "and to be gripped by fear is, I believe, the most degrading emotion for a human being." Disgusted by what he had seen in the first four years of the revolution, Sadat called on Nasser and told him that, while he would always be available as an advisor, he did not want a post in the new government. In Sadat's opinion, hate dominated the ruling group, and he wanted to keep his distance from it.

NATIONALIZATION AND EGYPTIANIZATION

A major turning point for Egypt came in the summer of 1956. On July 19, U.S. Secretary of State Dulles, declaring that the

Egyptian economy was bankrupt, withdrew offers that had been made by the U. S. and the World Bank to finance the building of the High Dam at Aswan. It was a direct and insulting slap at the Cairo government. Within days, the Soviet government informed Nasser that it would finance the High Dam project. His morale lifted sky-high, the Egyptian president was ready to take on the world. On July 26, he delivered a speech that stunned those who heard it. Egypt, he said, had nationalized the Suez Canal. The speech was shocking because the canal, built and owned by a British-French consortium, was one of those international institutions that seemed to be untouchable. The British and the French, of course, were aghast.

Sadat himself was stunned. Next day he told Nasser that he would have advised against the move at the time, since the Egyptian armed forces were not prepared for war. And Sadat was convinced that nationalization of the canal meant war. At the same time, he was proud that Egypt, a small, weak nation, had stood up to the powers of the western world. In the West, this intense nationalistic feeling was not understood. But to Sadat, the nationalization was a turning point in the history of Egypt; to the vast majority of Egyptians, Nasser had become an epic hero. After seventy-five years of humiliating subservience to the British, his countrymen were ready to idolize the man who dared to tweak the tail of the British lion.

But Sadat was right, of course, about the prospect of war. Anthony Eden, Premier Guy Mollet of France and Prime Minister David Ben-Gurion of Israel conspired to teach Egypt a lesson. To distract the Egyptian government, Britain and France engaged in negotiations with Egypt on compensation for the Suez stockholders. Then, on October 29, the three conspirators struck—Israeli troops invaded the Sinai, while British and French aircraft bombarded Egyptian military targets, destroying in one blow all the aircraft Egypt had bought from the Soviet Union. At the same time, tens of thousands of British and French airborne troops descended on Egypt, seizing key military points. In the thick of the fighting, Egypt asked the Soviet Union for emergency military aid, but Moscow refused point-blank. Already suspicious of the Soviets, Sadat was now convinced that it would be foolhardy to be totally reliant on such an undependable ally.

Help for the beleaguered Egyptians was to come from another, far different source: Dwight D. Eisenhower. The American president, though the nominal leader of the western alliance, had known nothing in advance about the strike against Egypt and he was deeply angered. On November 5, Eisenhower requested—really demanded—that the British, French and Israelis withdraw their troops from Egypt without delay. The three countries could do little but comply with the demand of their powerful ally and military protector. The British and the French withdrew their troops by December 23, their mission—to prevent the takeover of the Suez Canal by Egypt—a total failure. Israel, which at first had announced the annexation of the Sinai, pulled its forces out completely by March 1957.

After the French and British decided to heed Eisenhower's "request" that they get out of Egypt, the Soviet Union sent a warning to Paris and London threatening Soviet intervention. It was an empty piece of muscle-flexing, since Eisenhower had already put an end to the Anglo-French-Israeli adventure. President Nasser, however, chose to give credit to the Soviet Union for its help, ignoring the American role. Sadat was astonished, because he knew that the U.S. action had turned Egyptian defeat into victory. Moreover, he believed that Egypt should have used the occasion to strengthen relations with Washington, if only to frustrate Israeli strategy, which was to keep Egypt and the United States as far apart as possible. Sadat became convinced that Nasser's judgment was being warped by pro-Soviet advisors who flattered and cajoled a man who was increasingly taken with his own myth as a world leader.

On January 1, 1957, Nasser took another momentous step, declaring the "Egyptianization" of the country's economy. The move, made in retaliation for the damage caused by the Anglo-French air raids, was a serious blow to European investors. Until then, all insurance companies, banks and major business concerns were owned by French, British or other European interests. They naturally were unhappy about Nasser's action, although Sadat, in his memoirs, claimed that they received fair payment for their holdings, as did the shareholders in the old Suez Canal Company.

Egypt was now in control of its own economy; it had substantial assets and healthy revenues, in part due to Suez Canal tolls and in part to the seizure of company assets. In Sadat's opinion, Nasser should have immediately embarked on a vast program of domestic reconstruction. Unfortunately, no such program was undertaken. Nasser had little interest in problems of economic and social development at home. Instead, he became increasingly preoccupied with his image as an international figure, the hero who had defeated the armies of two great empires, the British and the French. Nasser came to believe that he, indeed, had defeated the invaders; he could never understand that he had been militarily defeated and that only Eisenhower had sent the invaders packing from Egypt.

MISTAKES AND SETBACKS

For Egypt, the late 1950's and most of the 1960's were painful years. In February 1958, Nasser let himself be talked into a merger between Egypt and Syria, a union called the United Arab Republic. Nasser was named president of the united country: Abdel Hakim Amer, with the rank of field marshal, assumed command of the joint armed forces. Sadat was later elected Speaker of the Federal (Syrian-Egyptian) National Assembly. From the start, it was widely predicted in the Arab world that such a union, entered into so casually, would eventually come to grief. The predictions were not long in coming true. By the summer of 1961, the Syrian people were fed up with Nasser and the socialist direction he introduced into their country. Moreover, the Syrian army was sick of taking orders from the Egyptians. In July, the Syrians arrested Amer in Damascus, bundled him aboard a plane and sent him back to Cairo. It was the end of the union, which was soon formally dissolved.

The ill-fated union with Syria had been bitterly opposed by the Soviet Union from the start, since Soviet strongman Nikita Khrushchev viewed any non-Communist grouping in the Middle East with undisguised hostility. This led to bad feelings between Nasser and Moscow, and in 1959 Nasser gave Sadat the green light to launch an anti-Soviet propaganda campaign. Sadat, then secretary-general of the National Union, the country's only legal political party, responded with enthusiasm. In speech after speech, he attacked the Soviets with unusual vigor, and later in life he was to recall that "I had unprecedented success in arousing anti-Soviet feeling." The enraged Nikita Khrushchev, noting that his country was Egypt's arms supplier, retorted with one of his peasant aphorisms: "Don't spit in your own well; you're bound to return to it for a drink."

Taking note of the coolness between Cairo and Moscow, the United States secretly offered to give Egypt whatever support it needed. But Nasser rejected the American overture, telling U.S. envoys that he would fight his own battles and that he just wanted the United States to help by supplying wheat and petroleum. At the time, American "Food for Peace" aid was a great help to the Egyptian economy, enabling it to function with reasonable success. When the grain shipments were stopped in 1965, the impact on the Egyptian economy was considerable. In Sadat's view, Nasser made a great mistake by not responding more positively to the American overture—if only to keep some balance in his relations with the two superpowers.

During the 1960's, Sadat increasingly became aware of aspects of Nasser's personality that he considered disturbing. He supported the president loyally, but he feared that Nasser was damaging the cause of the revolution by an extreme reliance on a coterie of self-seekers. His ego required flattery, and these people gave it to him in abundance. Nasser, normally the most supicious of men, seemed blind to the excesses committed by this group, supposedly in his behalf.

The greatest excesses, in Sadat's mind, were those of Nasser's friend, Abdel Hakim Amer. As commander in chief of the armed forces, Amer constantly enlarged his power, placing followers throughout the government apparatus. When, in 1965, it was learned that the fanatical Muslim Brotherhood was plotting to overthrow the regime, Nasser set up a "Committee for the Liquidation of Feudalism" and appointed Amer to head it. Soon it became clear that Amer and his henchmen were using brutal strong-arm methods, often against people who had nothing to do with the Muslim Brotherhood. They raided homes and arrested people in the middle of the night. They seized the property of their political opponents. Sadat also became convinced that they were using torture, and he clashed angrily with Amer over such tactics.

Sadat and others began to urge Nasser to remove Amer as commander in chief of the armed forces, and Nasser seemed to agree. But he could never bring himself to act against Amer—a failure that eventually would bring disaster to Egypt. Another war with Israel seemed inevitable. The Israelis had concentrated a powerful force on the Syrian border, and Egypt, which had a defense pact with Syria, beefed up its forces in the Sinai. Nasser's apparent aim was to deter an Israeli strike at Syria, but the situation got out of hand.

At the time, Nasser was under strong pressure from other Arab states to close the Strait of Tiran at the Gulf of Aqaba, Israel's only Red Sea outlet to international waters. Nasser called together his top advisors, including Amer and Sadat, and told them that the chances of war were fifty-fifty. If he closed the Tiran Strait, said Nasser, the chance of war would then be a hundred percent. Turning to Amer, Nasser asked if the armed forces were ready. Amer pointed to his neck and said: "On my own head be it, boss. Everything's in tip-top shape."

Reassured by Amer, Nasser closed the Tiran Strait and ordered the United Nations Emergency Forces stationed between Egyptian and Israeli forces in the Sinai to be withdrawn. War was now a certainty; Nasser, after endorsing a war plan, warned his commanders that the air force must be prepared for the first blow. On June 5, Amer flew off on an inspection tour over the Sinai, and with the commander in chief in the air, orders naturally were issued that all Egyptian antiaircraft batteries should hold their fire. At exactly that time, Israeli aircraft attacked Egypt's undefended airfields and all but wiped out the Egyptian air force on the ground. "We can thus say," Sadat commented bitterly, "that the war began and ended while Amer was in the air."

In the days that followed, the Israelis advanced across the Sinai, meeting with little resistance from Egyptian troops deprived of all air cover. Amer then ordered the total withdrawal of Egyptian forces to the west side of the canal, whereupon Nasser demanded to know why he did not try to establish a defense line at the Sinai Passes, a defensible line right down the middle of the peninsula. To Sadat's astonishment and disgust, Amer replied that the line—which should have been ready at all times—was *not* ready!

And so, the disaster for the Egyptians continued. By the 9th, the Israelis reached the eastern bank of the Suez, having taken all the major towns in the Sinai. "It's all over," Nasser

Egyptian troops in the Sinai prepare for an Israeli attack after President Nasser closed the Strait of Tiran in 1967.

told the dejected Sadat. Nasser then issued a statement saying that he was stepping down. In the days that followed, the people of Cairo—united in crisis—poured into the streets in a demonstration of support for Nasser. They demanded that he stay on as president, cursing the United States for its support of Israel in the crushing defeat, and threatening to burn the American embassy to the ground. On June 10, Sadat called on Nasser and pleaded with him to stay on. The people are determined to stand fast in the face of adversity, Sadat argued, and Nasser must do the same.

Nasser gave in and agreed to stay on, but clearly he was a broken man. In the days that followed, Sadat phoned Nasser several times, and each time the president's voice seemed weaker and more uncertain. His pride had been dealt a tremendous blow. Once a bold, defiant figure to many, especially in the Third World, he had been brought low by his enemies and by his own reliance on the likes of Amer.

END OF AN ERA

Nasser roused himself and made an effort to rebuild the Egyptian armed forces, while the Soviet Union increasingly frustrated him by holding off on arms deliveries, making it clear that Moscow and not Cairo was in charge of Egypt's military destiny. And, surprisingly, the problem of what to do about Amer still remained. Despite the military debacle, he not only refused to resign as commander in chief but actually defied Nasser to fire him and rallied hundreds of officers to support him. Nasser finally moved against his old friend, replacing him with Mahmouad Fawzi and arresting most of the pro-Amer officers. But Amer refused to give in. He continued to agitate against Nasser, distributing pamphlets critical of him and stockpiling weapons for an apparent coup attempt.

By now, Nasser was totally fed up. He summoned Amer to his home, and there, in the presence of a few trusted advisers, including Sadat, he confronted Amer with evidence of his disloyalty. Amer denied everything, but he was placed under house arrest and later removed to a detention center. Then, one evening, Sadat received a call from Nasser.

"Yes, Gamal, what's up?" asked Sadat.

"Abdel Hakim Amer has killed himself," replied a shaken Nasser.

That was the end of Amer's bid for power, but it was not the end of Nasser's troubles. Fearful of any sign of opposition, he tightened the regime's grip on power, issuing a statement on March 30, 1968, which upheld the government's right of arrest without charges and promised a permanent constitution only after the consequences of the 1967 defeat had been removed. The vast majority of Egyptians still backed Nasser, but rumblings of discontent were heard in many quarters about his increasingly dictatorial rule.

Still smarting over his overwhelming defeat at the hands of the Israelis, Nasser yearned for a measure of revenge. In September of 1968 he began the so-called "War of Attrition" against the Israeli forces in the occupied Sinai. Designed to wear down and demoralize the enemy, it opened with massive artillery barrages along the Suez Canal, then the dividing line between the Egyptians and the Israelis. The Israeli air force responded by smashing Egyptian power stations, bridges and factories, forcing Nasser to call off the War of Attrition for a time. It was resumed in March 1969, after the Egyptians had fortified their air defenses with additional Soviet-supplied SAM missiles, and for months thereafter the two sides inconclusively exchanged artillery and mortar barrages, commando raids and air strikes.

During this period, Sadat had deep disagreements with Nasser over the course of the revolution. He opposed the police-state aspects of the regime, and he thought that Nasser lacked flexibility and imagination in foreign affairs. Despite their disagreements, Nasser came to realize that Sadat, who put the good of Egypt above everything, was the one he

Sadat greets President Nasser (l.) whom he served
as a friend, adviser, and vice president.

trusted most. One day in December 1969, as Nasser was about to fly off to an Arab summit conference in Morocco, he turned to Sadat and commented on the intrigues that were constantly being hatched against him. He was convinced that one day the plotters would "get" him and, since he did not want to leave a vacuum behind, he had decided to name Sadat as his vice-president.

Sadat tried to refuse, telling Nasser he would be content to carry on as a friend and adviser. "Oh, no!" said Nasser. "You must be sworn in tomorrow." Next day, Sadat was indeed sworn in. At the airport, as he was about to leave for Morocco, Nasser announced the news to the press. Sadat, who had never sought power, was now second in command.

In his efforts to rebuild the Egyptian army, Nasser was repeatedly frustrated by the Soviet Union. Over and over, he begged the Soviets for additional help for Egypt's air defense and for additional offensive weaponry. But Moscow, annoyed because Nasser had started the War of Attrition without its approval, kept stalling him. By mid-1970, Nasser—who by then suffered from heart trouble, diabetes and excruciating leg pains—was a thoroughly beaten man. He told Sadat that the Soviet Union was a hopeless case as far as Egypt was concerned and that all the cards were in America's hands. It was high time, he said, that Egypt begin to improve its relations with the United States.

Shortly after this, the United States came up with the Rogers Plan, a proposal named after Secretary of State William Rogers. It provided for a ninety-day cease-fire in the War of Attrition, during which United Nations mediator Gunnar Jarring would conduct negotiations with all parties concerned for an overall settlement of the Middle East question. The Rogers Plan envisaged an Israeli withdrawal from the territories occupied in the 1967 War in exchange for an acceptance by the Arab states of Israel's sovereignty and territorial security.

By this time, Nasser realized that the Soviet Union could never provide a solution and he belatedly felt that nothing could be lost in playing the American card. In Moscow for a visit, Nasser told Soviet leader Leonid Brezhnev that he was ready to accept the Rogers Plan as a starting point for negotiations. Brezhnev became livid with rage at the possibility of an "American solution," but Nasser told him that he would accept anyone's solution if it worked—even one from the devil himself.

Nasser's acceptance of the Rogers Plan and his suspension of the War of Attrition earned him the intense hatred of the Palestine Liberation Organization, which saw even the possibility of an Egyptian peace with Israel as a betrayal. Bitter personal attacks on him by the PLO wounded Nasser deeply, since, in his opinion, he had done more than any other Arab leader to advance the cause of the Palestinians. In spite of the PLO's animosity, Nasser convened a summit conference in Cairo in September 1970, in an effort to put an end to the slaughter of PLO guerrillas then being carried out by the forces of King Hussein of Jordan. But for his efforts in behalf of the Palestinians, Nasser was subjected to fierce attacks from Libya's unpredictable Muammar Qaddafi and Yasir Arafat of the PLO. At the end of the conference, Nasser was so exhausted that he literally staggered to his car.

Nasser went home to rest after asking Sadat to join him for supper that evening. Sadat also went home and tried to get some sleep, only to be wakened by the telephone at 6:00 P.M. and asked to come to Nasser's house immediately. When he arrived, he was told that President Nasser was dead of a heart attack. Sadat insisted that the doctors keep trying to revive him, but the doctors assured him that they had done everything possible and that the will of God could not be reversed. Nasser was gone. His death was mourned by many millions of people throughout the Arab world.

SADAT TAKES COMMAND

5

Before Nasser's body was cold, a power struggle began in Cairo. Sadat, as the only vice-president, automatically became acting president. Rivals within the ruling Supreme Executive Committee of the Arab Socialist Union wanted to postpone a presidential election indefinitely in hopes of weakening Sadat's authority. But he insisted on prompt elections, and on October 15, 1970, Egyptians went to the polls and overwhelmingly endorsed Sadat as revolutionary Egypt's second president.

Following in the steps of the idolized Gamal Nasser, Sadat at first was perceived as a weak and unimpressive leader. Some of his colleagues derided him behind his back as "Nasser's poodle." Others ridiculed his well-tailored suits, his toothy grin and his seemingly hollow vows to punish Israel and redeem Egypt's military honor. Abroad, Sadat was regarded as a transitional figure. Elliot Richardson, whom President Nixon sent to attend Nasser's funeral, reported to Washington that Sadat could not last more than four to six weeks as president.

NASSER'S LEGACY

At the time, Richardson's forecast did not seem so foolish, for the situation Sadat inherited from Nasser was truly disastrous.

The country had recently suffered a humiliating military defeat; the economy was staggering; foreign policy was hobbled by a total dependence on the Soviet Union; the domestic political scene was marked by vicious intrigues and power plays. In an atmosphere of suspicion and hatred, Sadat's enemies in Cairo sharpened their knives in full expectation that the new president was ripe for a quick kill.

The world, including his Cairo enemies, badly underestimated Anwar Sadat. The poor village boy turned revolutionary, the dedicated nationalist who spent years in prison for his cause, was nobody's pushover. As president, he moved swiftly to establish himself as no carbon copy of Nasser. On his first day in office, he was presented with a pile of tapped personal telephone conversations, private discussions that had nothing to do with state affairs. Nasser, in his constant concern for security, had ordered the taps, but Sadat angrily swept them away. Then and there he ordered an end to all telephone tapping, except in cases of national security, and then only through a court order.

Sadat had established his concern for the rule of law and not rule by personal whim. In December, Sadat took an even more daring step, ending state custodianship—in reality, arbitrary seizure—of private property. Under custodianship, the property of individuals often had been taken over for no other reason than that their political views were at variance with those of important members of the government. In removing custodianship, Sadat won enthusiastic approval from most Egyptians—except, of course, those who had enjoyed the exercise of arbitrary power.

The economic mess bequeathed to Sadat was appalling. The Marxists around Nasser had convinced him that the private sector of the economy was an odious relic of capitalism, and as a consequence Nasser did all he could to stifle it. The public sector, which included all the state-run or state-controlled enterprises, was run by Moscow-oriented bureaucrats who thought that political slogans were a substitute for solid economic growth. Foreign confidence in the Egyptian economy was at low ebb; investment had dried up; the treasury was empty; the country verged dangerously close to bankruptcy. As a first step, Sadat insisted that his top economic advisors forget political rhetoric and concentrate on giving encouragement to the private sector. It would be many years, however, before the economic cobwebs gathered in the Nasser era were finally swept away.

In the realm of foreign affairs, Sadat inherited policies that had isolated Egypt from much of the world. Nasser was a man who thought in terms of "black and white." No gray shadings were permitted. To him, the world was neatly divided between good "progressive" and bad "reactionary" countries. By definition, the wealthy kingdoms and sheikdoms of the Arab world fell into the reactionary category, and his relations with them were decidedly strained. And if Cairo had few close friends in the Arab world, its relations with Europe and the United States were in tatters. Egypt's only important "friend," the Soviet Union, was far more interested in consolidating its presence in the Middle East and in backing its supporters in Cairo than in helping Egypt solve its economic and military problems.

In March 1971, Sadat made his first visit to Moscow as president. In heated sessions with the Soviet leadership, including Leonid Brezhnev, Sadat insisted that the Soviets supply the SAM missiles they had promised Nasser, make up for Egypt's losses in ammunition during the War of Attrition, and provide Egypt with advanced aircraft. The Soviets promised Sadat the SAM's and the ammunition, and Brezhnev offered to send Egypt advanced, missile-equipped aircraft and to train Egyptian crews to use them. There was, however, a catch: the planes could not be used unless Moscow gave its okay. Sadat flatly rejected the offer, telling the Soviet leaders that "nobody is allowed to take a decision on Egyptian affairs except the people of Egypt itself—represented by me, the President of Egypt."

Back in Cairo, Sadat informed the Supreme Executive Council about his talks in Moscow. When he told how he had turned down the offer of advanced aircraft because of the strings attached, his pro-Soviet opponents barely managed to contain their anger. They left the room seething. It would not be long, Sadat thought, before they would move against him.

Sadat decided to move first. He removed Ali Sabri, who had close ties to the Soviet Union, from a leadership position, and bluntly informed the Soviet ambassador that he no longer had a "man in Cairo." Information reaching Sadat convinced him that Sabri, secret police chief Sharawi Gomah and others were plotting to kill him and seize control of the government. On May 13, he dismissed Gomah, triggering a group resignation from the top levels of the government by members of the Sabri-Gomah clique. They had hoped to precipitate a political crisis by their action, but Sadat did not lose his nerve. He crisply accepted the resignations, made the news public and placed the entire group under house arrest. That very night, Sadat transformed the government, replacing the ousted plotters with new men whose allegiance, he believed, was first and foremost to Egypt.

Sadat's action in ridding the government of people associated with the harsher aspects of Nasser's rule was immensely popular. It was a demonstration of one of Sadat's strengths, an intuitive grasp of what the people wanted. On May 15, he took another important step toward the dismantling of the police state, ordering that the tapes of people's private telephone conversations held by the Interior Ministry be burned, that all detention centers for political prisoners be closed down, and that arbitrary arrests be halted. Sadat regarded these actions as the first steps in the construction of a different kind of socialist state—one characterized by genuine social justice rather than empty Marxist slogans.

DEALING WITH MOSCOW

In late May 1971, after the arrest of his pro-Soviet rivals, Sadat received a visit from Nikolai Podgorny, a powerful member of the Soviet Politburo. Podgorny explained that Moscow strongly desired a Treaty of Friendship and Co-operation between Egypt and the Soviet Union. To mollify the Russians and keep them guessing about his true intentions, Sadat agreed. Podgorny thereupon pulled out a treaty drafted in Moscow and Sadat signed it. But treaty or no treaty, the gap between Sadat and the Russians continued to widen. Podgorny promised Sadat an immediate supply of new weapons; they never came, and Moscow ignored Sadat's strenuous complaints. When Communists attempted a coup in neighboring Sudan, Sadat opposed it vehemently, asserting that Egypt would not tolerate a Communist regime on its border. The coup failed, and the disappointed Soviets did not forgive Sadat for his anti-Communist stand.

Sadat had promised that 1971 would be the "year of decision," in which real progress toward a Middle East settlement with Israel would be made, either through diplomacy or war. He surprised the world by suddenly offering to negotiate a peace treaty if Israel would try to settle the Palestine refugee problem and withdraw to pre-1967 borders. It was a radical move for an Arab leader, but Israel rejected it and the United States all but ignored it. In October, Sadat again visited Moscow, where he was promised additional arms, including missile-equipped aircraft. This time the Soviets did not insist that the aircraft be used only with their approval. But the Soviets, who wanted Sadat to know that he was dependent on them for arms and who did not want him to go to war with

Israel again, held back on deliveries. As a result, the unhappy Sadat had to postpone his Year of Decision.

In February 1972, Sadat once again went to Moscow, in hopes of getting the Soviets to send the arms they had promised. As usual, Brezhnev and his colleagues agreed to send weapons; not the ones Sadat wanted, but arms nevertheless. In May of that year, however, détente was in the air. President Richard Nixon visited Moscow, and a communique issued by Nixon and Brezhnev called for a military relaxation in the Middle East. To Sadat, "relaxation" was a code-word for acceptance of Israel's victory and the conquests of 1967.

The Soviet Union continued to be evasive about the promised arms shipments, and finally Sadat's patience wore out. In July 1972, Sadat caused a worldwide sensation when he suddenly ordered the fifteen thousand Soviet military experts in Egypt to leave the country within a week. The exasperated Sadat also ordered that Soviet equipment in Egypt either be sold to Egypt or withdrawn within the same time period. The Soviets refused to sell four advanced MIG-25 aircraft stationed in Egypt or their electronic jamming equipment. By the end of the week, the equipment, and the experts, were flown back to the Soviet Union.

Sadat's decision to oust the Russians was caused in part by their attempts to use arms supplies as a means of controlling Egyptian policy. Another important cause was Moscow's arrogant attitude toward Egypt and its contempt for Egyptian military prowess. As Sadat admitted, he wanted to put the Soviet Union in its place—just as he once had wanted to put the British Raj in its place. He wanted to tell the Russians, and the world, that the will of Egypt was entirely Egyptian.

PREPARATION FOR BATTLE

Most concerned parties, the Soviet Union, the West and Israel, misinterpreted Sadat's motives in throwing out the

Soviet experts. They thought that by throwing out the Russians Sadat was giving up all thought of another war with Israel. Sadat did not see it that way. He felt that the Soviets—who believed that Egypt could never successfully challenge Israel militarily—were trying to rein him back from another war. Sadat still preferred a diplomatic solution, but neither Israel nor its patron America seemed to feel any urgency about a settlement. "The time has come for a shock," Sadat said in an interview. "The resumption of the battle is now inevitable."

At first, Sadat decided on November 15, 1972, as the date for an attack on Israeli forces in the Sinai. But as his war minister proved to be hopelessly incompetent, and units of the armed forces were not made ready for battle in time, Sadat once again postponed his struggle to regain Egypt's lost territory. It was a wise move. He named a highly intelligent officer, Maj. Gen. Ahmed Ismail Ali, as war minister and commander in chief of the armed forces. In short order, Ali—later raised to the rank of marshal—completed defense preparations, which had been totally neglected by his predecessor, and began work on an offensive plan.

The expulsion of the Soviet military experts had placed a severe strain on relations between Cairo and Moscow. But Sadat still needed Soviet arms. And the Soviets, despite their humiliation, were not yet ready to abandon their political and economic investment in the most important country in the Arab world. In March, 1973, Sadat sent Ali to Moscow, where the war minister successfully negotiated the biggest Soviet-Egyptian arms deal yet. To Sadat's surprise, some of those arms actually arrived on schedule; other weapons, in the usual Soviet fashion, were held back until later, when they were no longer needed.

In preparation for the battle, Sadat bolstered his ties with the Arab world and with Third World nations who sympathized with his goal of driving the Israelis out of Egyptian territory. He conferred secretly with Syrian President Hafez al-

Assad to co-ordinate a joint military campaign against the Israelis. Together, Sadat and Assad set the attack for October 6—Yom Kippur, the Jewish Day of Atonement—when all public services would be suspended in Israel.

In May and August, Sadat ordered civil defense measures that tricked the Israelis into thinking that a military move was imminent. On both occasions, the Israelis felt obliged to order a full military mobilization. But Sadat was not yet ready to move. During the summer months, he paid visits to many military units, encouraging a martial spirit among the soldiers. The impending battle, he told them, would not be easy. The Egyptians would have to attack across a water barrier, the Suez Canal, and then penetrate the 47-foot (14-m) high Israeli earthworks and the supposedly impregnable Bar-Lev Line. The latter was a highly sophisticated and strongly defended line named after Israeli General Chaim Bar-Lev. But, Sadat said to his soldiers, if Egyptian troops could cross the canal into the Sinai and liberate even a portion of Egyptian lands, the humiliation of the 1967 defeat would be erased.

In late September, final training exercises were completed by the Egyptian ground and air forces, while naval units sailed out to their combat stations. On October 1, Sadat signed the war order; things were in readiness. The Soviet government, when told on October 3 of the war plan, showed a total lack of confidence in the Egyptians, hastily flying Soviet civilians out of Egypt and diverting arms-laden ships from Egyptian ports. But Sadat, convinced that Egypt was ready for the fight, was relaxed and confident. He looked forward to October 6, when Egypt—he prayed—would regain not only its land but its military honor.

THE OCTOBER WAR

At 2:00 P.M. sharp on October 6, according to plan, over two hundred Egyptian supersonic jets roared across the canal and struck at Israeli positions. The attack achieved near-total surprise and near-total success. Within twenty minutes, the Egyptian jets smashed Israeli command posts, air combat headquarters, air defense and jamming centers, missile batteries and gun emplacements in the Sinai. An estimated 90 percent of the planned targets were hit and only a handful of aircraft were lost. In that first stunning wave, the Israelis were badly battered; their military communications were smashed, as they would remain for several days.

The air strike was followed by a devastating artillery barrage—the heaviest unleashed anywhere since World War II. Then came the crucial dangerous crossing of the canal by Egyptian soldiers in a thousand small rubber assault boats. The first to cross to the East Bank scaled the Israeli earthworks and then let down rope ladders for their comrades; soon they took a number of Israeli positions behind the earthworks and provided cover for further landings. The first large unit to cross was the Egyptian Seventh Brigade, and in the Operations Room in Cairo the joyful Sadat and his military commanders received word that the Egyptian flag flew over the East Bank once again.

When the first troops had crossed, army engineers began to carve out passes in the earthworks with extremely high-powered water pumps. The water cut through the sandy earthworks with ease, creating huge gaps, through which Egyptian tanks—having crossed the canal on quickly erected pontoon bridges—rolled into the Israeli-occupied Sinai. By nightfall, five full Egyptian armored divisions had successfully crossed, along 110 miles (177 km) of the canal, to the East Bank of the Suez. In the onslaught, strongpoint after strongpoint in the vaunted Bar-Lev defensive line fell to the Egyptians.

That very evening, the Soviet ambassador to Egypt asked Sadat to agree to a cease-fire within forty-eight hours. Sadat refused, saying that he would not hear of a cease-fire until his main objectives had been achieved. In the days that

Egyptian troops cross a hastily erected bridge to the East Bank of the Suez Canal during the October War in 1973.

followed, the Soviets—still convinced that the Egyptians would eventually be defeated—persistently tried to get Sadat's assent to a cease-fire. He continued to reject the idea. Instead, he demanded that the Soviets rush him some new tanks, since the biggest tank battle in history—bigger than any in World War II—was unfolding in the Sinai. Before the Sinai battle was over, perhaps five thousand tanks took part in the action.

At first, the outside world had difficulty believing Egyptian reports of victories over the Israelis. But from the third day on, it became clear to everyone that the Israelis were in serious trouble. In those first three days, Israel lost one-third of its air force on the Syrian and Egyptian fronts. The Syrians made small advances in the Golan Heights area, and the Egyptians inflicted heavy losses on crack Israeli tank units in the Sinai. Egyptian tanks took substantial losses, too, but the tide was running strongly in favor of the Egyptians. Israel Defense Minister Moshe Dayan, in a state of shock, declared publicly that the road to Tel Aviv was open to the Egyptians.

The demoralized Dayan offered his resignation, which was rejected by Prime Minsiter Golda Meir. As she later wrote, the early days of the October War were "a near disaster, a nightmare that I experienced and which will always be with me."

In Washington, the U.S. government, Israel's staunchest supporter, began to fear the worst. On the fourth day of the war, with the battle in the Sinai raging on, Washington received an emergency request from Israel for four hundred tanks to make up for their losses. At the same time, U.S. military intelligence reported to the Nixon Administration that the war was not going well for the Israelis. When this began to sink in, U.S. officials—especially Secretary of State Henry Kissinger—started to work for a cease-fire. First, Kissinger called for a cease-fire based on the pre-war lines of October 6; then, when he realized that Israel was faced with total defeat, he called for a cease-fire on the lines of October 13, lines which reflected Egypt's gains in the first week of battle. Sadat, however, refused to accept a cease-fire until Israel agreed to withdraw from the Arab territories it seized in the 1967 war.

After their initial setbacks, the Israelis struck back fiercely. They flung back the Syrians, inflicting heavy losses. They launched punishing air strikes on Egyptian installations and cities close to the West Bank of the canal. Driving through Egyptian lines in the Sinai, Israeli tanks and infantry crossed onto the West Bank of the Suez. As the Israeli bridgehead slowly expanded, some Egyptian military men advised Sadat to withdraw his troops from the East Bank in order to protect Egypt's cities. But he refused, convinced that Egypt could contain the Israeli thrust and eventually trap the Israelis who had crossed the canal. At the very least, however, the Israelis had succeeded in thoroughly confusing the military picture.

To add a further complication, Sadat was becoming deeply concerned about the growing role of the United States in the fighting. After the White House became convinced that Israel was in danger of defeat, it ordered that a U.S. satellite transmit hourly information to the Israelis on the disposition of enemy forces. In addition, the United States began to rush in new equipment in an effort to "save Israel" and turn defeat into victory. Directly behind the front, at Al-Arish, capital of the Sinai, huge American transport planes disgorged hundreds of new tanks and advanced weapons not seen in the region until that time. One experimental weapon, a U.S. rocket called the TV-camera bomb, immediately took a toll, knocking out Egyptian missile batteries with devastating accuracy. It was obvious to Sadat that the American weapon could soon destroy his entire defense system, thus giving the Israeli air force "open skies" over Egypt.

On October 19, Sadat decided to accept a cease-fire. He had come to the conclusion that the United States would spare neither effort nor money to prevent an Israeli defeat and that he could not, in his words, "fight the entire United States of America." When he thought of American aid to Israel, Sadat was bitter about the grudging support given to Egypt by the Soviet Union during the fighting. The Soviets refused to give Egypt military information gathered by their satellites; their resupply of lost equipment was slow and insufficient. The Israelis and the Americans were determined to defeat Egypt, Sadat reflected, while the Soviets—still angry over his expulsion of their military experts—were lukewarm supporters of the Egyptian cause.

THE CEASE-FIRE

Prodded by Washington and Moscow, the United Nations Security Council finally got both sides to agree that a cease-fire should take effect at 7:00 P.M. on October 22. Between the 19th and the 22nd, however, the fighting continued, with Israeli troops in the West Bank bridgehead taking heavy casualties. Then, at the appointed time on October 22, Sadat ordered Egyptian military operations to cease. But after the cease-fire came into being, the Israeli forces on the West Bank sent columns of troops racing toward the Egyptian cities of Suez and Ismailia. They failed in their attempt to seize those cities, but they did extend their position on the West Bank and encircled the Egyptian Third Army.

Sadat was outraged by the Israeli violation of the cease-fire, which he saw as an attempt to gain bargaining leverage and as a last-minute attempt to save face. In meetings with Kissinger, he told the American that, if the Israelis did not withdraw to the lines of October 22, he would resume military operations and annihilate the Israeli pocket on the West Bank. If Sadat attempted to do that, Kissinger warned, the United States would intervene on the Israeli side.

As Sadat pondered this reality, United Nations-sponsored talks on a disengagement of forces and a return to the cease-fire lines of October 22 began at a crossroads on the Cairo-Suez road. The haggling went on until late December, when Sadat and his military commanders decided on a plan to liquidate the Israeli pocket on the West Bank and relieve the Third Army. Kissinger, however, was now making progress with the Israelis on a disengagement agreement and pleaded with Sadat not to renew hostilities. As Kissinger recalls in *Years of Upheaval*, the second volume of his memoirs, he explained to Sadat that he was working for a "genuine disengagement of forces" that would go beyond the cease-fire lines of October 22 by moving Israeli troops back across the canal and guaranteeing Egyptian control of the East Bank. If it could be negotiated, Kissinger argued, "it would be the first Israeli withdrawal from Arab territory occupied for any length of time; it would create the confidence for further steps."

Sadat lapsed into silence for some minutes. Then, puffing on his pipe, the Egyptian calmly agreed that Kissinger was on the right track and that he should proceed with his negotiations with Israel. Sadat's gamble in allowing the United States to assume a mediator's role for the first time, a gamble opposed by all his advisors, eventually paid off. On January 18, 1974, Egypt and Israel signed a document worked out by the U.S. Secretary of State. Israeli troops withdrew from the West Bank of the Suez; limited numbers of Egyptian troops occupied a strip 5 to 7.5 miles (8 to 12 km) wide along the East Bank of the canal from the Mediterranean to the Gulf of Suez; and forces of the United Nations manned a buffer zone 3.5 to 5 miles (5 to 8 km) deep separating Israeli and Egyptian units. Once again, Egypt occupied both banks of the canal.

Both sides had suffered heavy casualties in the October War. But despite the last-minute efforts of the Israelis, Sadat felt able to claim a victory. Conservatively estimated, Israel had lost 2,500 soldiers (a per capita figure comparable to a loss of over 150,000 by a country the size of the United States). The cost of destroyed Israeli equipment was estimated at $2 billion. The losses to the Israeli economy, due to mobilization and fighting, were put at $7 billion.

Psychologically, there could be little question that Sadat had scored an enormous victory. Egypt had destroyed the myth of Israeli invincibility and demonstrated the ability of its own armed forces. The disgrace of 1967 was wiped out. Egyptians felt proud again, and the world began to take a fresh look at the power realities in the Middle East. Now that Sadat had proven that Egypt was capable of exercising a military option, he could turn to the even more difficult task of seeking peace with Israel.

FOR THE SAKE
OF PEACE

6

In the weeks after the October War, the Arab world briefly rallied around Sadat. Kings and sheikhs and radicals all met in Algiers in November 1973, and listened respectfully to Sadat's proposals for a comprehensive peace settlement with Israel. Sadat, aided by Syrian President Hafez Assad, convinced the hotter heads at the summit that an immediate return to war with Israel would be a serious blunder. In the end, "Sadat's war" seemed to have accomplished the impossible: a large degree of Arab unity. The summit approved a continuation of the oil embargo—which had been imposed by the oil-producing Arab nations during the October War—on shipments to countries supporting Israel. The Arab leaders also agreed to attend a peace conference in Geneva, sponsored by the United States and the Soviet Union, that would address the entire range of Middle East problems.

The appearance of unity in the Arab camp was not to last long. Sadat tried to convert some of the other leaders to his theory that only the United States had the power and influence to secure concessions from Israel. No other power, he argued, could mediate between two sides separated by such a barrier of hatred and suspicion. The radicals among the Arab leaders refused to accept the fact that the United States held the high cards in the Middle East power game.

They began to distance themselves from the Egyptian leader as he edged toward friendship with the United States. The radical leaders were joined by Syria's President Assad, who was a personal friend of Sadat but totally dependent on the Soviet Union for arms and aid.

In Egypt, Sadat's popularity soared to unprecedented heights as a result of the October War. But the war did not long divert the attention of the Egyptian people from their dreadful poverty or from the economic woes of the country at large. The economic mess inherited by Sadat had not yet been cleaned up. Discontent—particularly with food prices— was widespread in Cairo and other cities. Sadat, more than ever, realized that the nation's resources had to be channeled away from war and into the crippled economy.

NEW HORIZONS

Well before the October War, Sadat had made peace overtures to Israel. Soon after becoming president in October 1970, he had refused—against the advice of many high Egyptian officials—to renew the War of Attrition against Israel. In November, when the cease-fire that was part of the Rogers Plan was about to expire, he had extended it for ninety days. When that extension came to an end in February 1971, Sadat—though in office little more than three months— felt that he had to take constructive action that would prove to the world that he wanted peace with Israel. Accordingly, he had made his remarkable "Initiative for Peace," in which he offered peace and security to Israel in exchange for withdrawal from conquered Arab territories.

It was the first time that an Arab leader had dared to suggest making peace with Israel. The proposal won worldwide approval; the people of Egypt—except for Sadat's proSoviet enemies—were enthusiastic in their support. William Rogers, the U.S. Secretary of State at the time, welcomed the

*President Sadat welcomes Secretary of State
Henry Kissinger during Kissinger's efforts
to negotiate a disengagement agreement
between Egypt and Israel in November 1973.*

initiative as a highly positive step. Unfortunately, the Israeli government of Prime Minister Golda Meir thought otherwise. Unwilling to give up an inch of the Sinai, Mrs. Meir refused to entertain Sadat's proposal and even rebuked Rogers publicly for daring to raise the proposal with her. There was no will to make peace in the Meir government, Sadat concluded. Had the United States exerted more pressure on Israel to take the Initiative for Peace more seriously, the October War of 1973—a costly one for Israel—would never have occurred.

After the October War, Henry Kissinger, who had replaced Rogers as Secretary of State, met with Sadat and with him embarked on what they called a "peace process." There was an immediate rapport between the two men. Wrote Sadat in his memoirs: "For the first time, I felt as if I was looking at the real face of the United States, the one I had always wanted to see." The two were soon on a "Henry" and "Anwar" basis. Kissinger, the master of *realpolitik*, quickly realized that he was face to face with someone out of the ordinary. "His negotiating tactic was never to haggle over detail but to create an atmosphere that made disagreement psychologically difficult," Kissinger recalled in *White House Years*, the first volume of his memoirs. "I cannot say that I fully understood Sadat's insight then. Great men are so rare that they take some getting used to."

Sadat's new relationship with the United States was looked on with the greatest suspicion by the Soviet Union. For years, Moscow had considered Egypt to be in its sphere of influence. Now, after Sadat's defeat of the pro-Soviet opposition in Egypt, his expulsion of the Soviet experts, his vocal opposition to the attempted Communist takeover in the Sudan, and his decision to go to war against Israel over Soviet objections, the Soviet Union had to swallow another bitter pill: his determination to work with Kissinger to achieve a comprehensive Middle East peace. After Sadat's intentions became clear to Moscow, it shut off all arms supplies and adopted an openly hostile attitude.

Shuttling between Cairo and Jerusalem, Kissinger produced two agreements—one in 1974, the other in 1975—disengaging Egyptian and Israeli troops in the Sinai. But the overall peace process—with its hope for a full peace—appeared to be stymied. In an effort to stir up some diplomatic movement, Sadat decided on a dramatic step: the reopening of the Suez Canal. The international waterway had been closed to shipping since the 1967 War and the occupation by Israeli troops of its East Bank. Under the first disengagement agreement, Israeli troops had withdrawn a short distance from the canal, but their big guns still were in firing range. Sadat, nevertheless, took the chance. On June 5, 1975, he declared the canal open, sailed through it on the Egyptian destroyer *October 6*, and allowed evacuees to return to the three canal towns of Suez, Ismailia and Port Said. To the world, the reopening of the canal demonstrated Sadat's deep commitment to peace and normalization in the Middle East.

THE ROAD TO JERUSALEM

Despite the efforts of Sadat and Kissinger, diplomacy stagnated for a time as Israel and the United States struggled to overcome domestic difficulties. Under attack for Israel's shaky performance in the early stages of the October War, Golda Meir stepped down as Prime Minister of Israel in April 1974, and was replaced by Yitzhak Rabin, a former army chief of staff and ambassador to Washington. Rabin, who headed a fragile coalition that included members of the right-wing Likud Party, was politically far too weak to fully pursue the peace process with Egypt. Rabin was replaced as head of the ruling Labor Party by Shimon Peres in early 1977, and in May of that year Labor—which had governed Israel since its inception—was soundly defeated at the polls by Likud. Its hard-line leader, Menachem Begin, became prime minister—a development that was seen at the time as a major setback for the cause of peace between Israel and the Arabs.

In the United States, the disintegration of the Nixon Administration and the uncertain interim presidency of Gerald Ford seriously undermined Kissinger's diplomatic efforts. But Sadat did not despair. After Jimmy Carter became president of the United States in January, 1977, Sadat was determined to build a close relationship with the Georgian. From the first, he impressed on Carter his desire for a peace with Israel that encompassed Israel's withdrawal from Arab territories, a solution to the Palestine problem, and full recognition of Israel. Sadat also made it clear that he understood Israel's need for security and that firm security guarantees should be part of any peace agreement.

Sadat and Carter corresponded frequently, and the two men—both deeply religious, both with roots in the soil—came to respect and trust each other. Carter understood the tremendous psychological barrier—the huge wall of hatred and suspicion—that separated the Arabs and Israelis. In one letter, the American president explored the whole complicated skein of Middle East problems, and that letter, as Sadat later stated, indirectly caused him to embark on a completely fresh reappraisal of his own. The time had come, Sadat thought, for a new approach, and in his mind he returned to the seclusion of Cell 54, where he had discovered that he possessed what many others do not: a capacity for making a profound change in his outlook. As he wrote: "He who cannot change the very fabric of his thought will never be able to change reality, and will never, therefore, make any progress."

Puffing on his pipe as he took solitary walks along the Nile, Sadat reexamined all aspects of the Arab-Israeli question. For a generation, Arabs had been brought up to regard Israel as taboo, an entity to be dealt with only on the battlefield. The Israelis felt the same way about the Arabs. Sadat wondered whether those attitudes could not be altered and whether something could not be done to tear down the barrier of mutual mistrust. Sadat was further encouraged in his hope for a new approach to peace during a visit with President Nicolae Ceausescu of Rumania in early October 1977. Ceausescu, the only leader in Communist eastern Europe to maintain cordial ties with Israel, had seen Israeli Prime Minister Menachem Begin a few weeks earlier. Now, in his meeting with Sadat, the Rumanian offered his opinion that Begin, despite his reputation as a hard-liner, was genuinely interested in finding a peace settlement. Not only that, said Ceausescu, Begin was strong enough to lead Israel in the direction of peace.

Back in Cairo, Sadat continued to ponder. One day, almost as if in a vision, he saw himself praying at al-Aqsa Mosque in Jerusalem, the third holiest Muslim shrine after Mecca and Medina. It suddenly became clear to Sadat that he might achieve a breakthrough by making a personal visit to Jerusalem and facing the Israelis in the center of their camp, despite the fact that the two countries were still in a state of war. It was an incredible thought! In November, Sadat acted on his decision, declaring to the People's Assembly that he would "go to the ends of the earth," even the Israeli Knesset (Parliament), for peace.

Fellow Arabs, including many of Sadat's friends, thought that the remark was purely a mental slip, something mistakenly uttered in the heat of oratory. But he assured them that he was in dead earnest. The Israelis were equally stunned by Sadat's speech, but they recovered quickly and on November 17 the U.S. ambassador called on the Egyptian president and handed him an official invitation from Prime Minister Begin to visit Jerusalem. After so many years of glacially-slow movement, events were now moving with amazing swiftness. "I am going to Jerusalem," Sadat told skeptics, "and the others

(Arab leaders) will have to follow in line." Just before Sadat took off for Jerusalem on the 19th, one of his aides shook his head and remarked: "Either this man is mad, or he is truly great."

Less than forty minutes after taking off from Abu Suwayr airport in the canal region, Sadat landed at Lod airport in Israel. A new chapter was about to unfold. On hand to greet the Egyptian president was a Who's Who of Israeli political life: former Prime Minister Golda Meir, former Prime Minister Yitzhak Rabin, former Defense Minister Moshe Dayan, conspicuous with his black eyepatch, former Foreign Minister Abba Eban, and General Ariel Sharon, the cocky general who led the Israeli counterattack in the October War. In his book *The Rabin Memoirs*, Rabin vividly described the scene:

"I confess that as I stood on the receiving line waiting for President Sadat's plane to land, I was possessed by a strange feeling. Even though I had participated in negotiations with Egypt in 1949, subsequent events had reinforced an idea that had been with me since my youth—that Egypt was the enemy. And even though, during my term as Prime Minister, we had done everything possible to move closer to peace, I cannot say that I really expected Egypt's head of state to visit Israel, openly, and with all the pomp and formal ceremonies, at such an early date. As the plane taxied up to the reception area and the door opened, the tension of the crowd waiting at the airport began to soar. But when President Sadat appeared in the doorway and moved out to the top of the steps, our emotion peaked in a way I had not thought possible. It was a uniquely electric moment for us all; one of those moments that remain etched in your memory forever; the kind that people call upon to date a generation . . . As the national anthems were played by the Israeli military band, and especially when President Sadat followed his military escort to review the honor guard of the Israeli Defense Forces, I felt that I was caught up in a dream. Despite the evidence of my own eyes and ears, what was happening around me seemed quite unbelievable."

What happened next day must have seemed even more unbelievable. Sadat said his prayers at al-Aqsa Mosque, then went to the Knesset to deliver his speech. The audience of parliamentarians was hushed and totally attentive. The event was televised, and many Israelis wept as Sadat said: "You would like to live with us in this region of the world, and I tell you in all honesty that we welcome you among us." But he bluntly told his listeners that peace must be based on justice. Israel must withdraw from all the Arab territories it conquered in the 1967 war, including Arab Jerusalem, and recognize the "fundamental rights" of the Palestinians, including their "right to establish their own state." In exchange, Sadat held out the promise of peace and "all the international guarantees you envisage and accept . . . from the two superpowers or from either of them . . . any guarantees you accept."

When he concluded the historic speech with the Arabic words *Salaam Aleikum*—peace be upon you—the Knesset gave him an enthusiastic ovation. Israeli soldiers, there to guard Sadat, scarcely contained their joy as they saluted him. He had made a truly remarkable offer, one which no other Arab leader had dared to think let alone utter, in ringing tones to the world. Sadat even disarmed many skeptical Israelis when he openly recognized Israel's need for security. Wrote Rabin: "The mere fact that an Arab leader who had waged war against Israel came forth and stated that he understood our need for security and that a way must be found to meet our legitimate concern was absolutely revolutionary."

ACCORD AT CAMP DAVID

On his arrival home in Cairo, Egyptians gave Sadat a tumultuous welcome. "All barriers of doubt, mistrust and fear have

*Egyptian President Sadat addresses the Israeli
Knesset on his historic trip to Jerusalem in 1977.*

President Sadat, President Carter, and Prime Minister
Begin join in a three-way handshake following the
signing of a peace treaty between Egypt and Israel.

been shattered," he told his countrymen. The People's Assembly endorsed his actions, with only a handful out of 360 registering an objection.

Beyond question, Sadat's visit to Jerusalem was a major milestone in the modern history of the Middle East. But in the months that followed, negotiations with the Israelis bogged down over many issues, particularly the question of the Palestinians and their future. The deadlock continued until September 1978, when President Carter gathered Sadat and Begin together at the presidential retreat at Camp David, Maryland. It was, by any standard, an uncommon event. The born-again Baptist president practically imprisoned the Muslim and Jewish heads of state for eleven days. They argued, they haggled—and they prayed.

In the end, the three men achieved something quite remarkable: the framework of a peace treaty between Egypt and Israel. Basically, Sadat, Begin and Carter agreed that Israel would withdraw from the entire Sinai peninsula, which it captured during the 1967 War, and that Egypt would develop full peaceful relations with its former enemy. The withdrawal would be phased over a three-year period, and each stage of it would be accompanied by Egyptian moves—such as opening the border to tourists and exchanging ambassadors—to broaden links between the two countries. (In addition, Egypt and Israel agreed to work toward Palestinian "autonomy" on the West Bank of the Jordan and Gaza.) Both sides realized that the degree of autonomy the Israelis would eventually relinquish to the Palestinians would be a thorny problem. But vague as the agreement was, it was important. It implied that Israel was committed to at least a modicum of Palestinian self-rule, and it supported Egypt's contention that it had not abandoned the Palestinian cause by making peace with Israel.

At the end of their stay at Camp David, the three leaders

were an astonishing sight, smiling broadly, bantering and even hugging each other for the television cameras. "(Our) prayers have been answered," said President Carter. Details of a formal treaty remained to be ironed out, and this work went on for months. Finally, in March 1979, Carter flew to Jerusalem and Cairo with proposals for breaking the deadlock. Both sides accepted them, and later that month on the White House lawn in Washington Sadat and Begin signed the treaty that put an end to thirty years of Egyptian-Israeli confrontation. "Let us work together," said Sadat, paraphrasing the prophet Isaiah, "until the day comes when they beat their swords into plowshares and their spears into pruning hooks."

THE CAULDRON OF FANATICISM

7

To much of the world, Sadat the peacemaker was a heroic figure, a rare individual who, by an act of will, changed the tide of history. After the peace treaty with Israel, the Egyptian president was lionized in the West and much sought after for magazine interviews and television appearances. Those who met him, including his former Israeli enemies, were often charmed by his grace and friendliness. "He immediately created a relationship of sincerity, friendship, frankness and warmth," recalled former Deputy Israeli Prime Minister Yigel Yadin, "and in this way he was like a member of the family."

Even the trivia of Sadat's personal life became of intense interest to millions. Apart from a weakness for well-cut suits and Dunhill pipe tobacco imported from England, his tastes were simple. He ate only one meal a day, and he sometimes fasted for days; he often spent evenings watching private screenings of American westerns with his wife Jihan. Preferring to deal with the broad issues, he left detailed paperwork, which he detested, to his subordinates. Sadat disliked official documents and insisted on verbal reports. When U.S. Secretary of State Cyrus Vance brought him Jimmy Carter's invitation to Camp David, Sadat asked Vance to read it to him aloud.

For all his outgoing charm, Sadat was an intensely private man. He never attended purely social occasions, and on a visit to the United States he had to refuse an offer by singer Pearl Bailey to dance with him. He had never learned to dance, he explained apologetically. When visitors, even important ones, came to see him, Sadat often lapsed into long periods of silence. At his summer retreat near the Libyan border, he once told U.S. Ambassador Hermann Eilts: "I have to think about something very quietly." He sat there, recalled Eilts, puffing on his pipe and filling the room with tobacco smoke. The ambassador did not know whether to leave or stay. Finally, after forty-five minutes of reflection, Sadat picked up the thread of the conversation.

ISOLATION IN THE ARAB WORLD

But if Sadat was admired in many parts of the world, his standing among many of his fellow Arabs was questionable. Enraged by his peace treaty with Israel, seventeen Arab countries imposed political and economic sanctions against Egypt. To them, the abandonment of the struggle against Israel was not statesmanship but something akin to treason; to the Palestine Liberation Organization, Sadat became an enemy who had sold out their cause to achieve a separate peace for Egypt. Left-wing Arabs particularly hated Sadat for his hostility toward the Soviet Union and friendship for the United States.

Had Sadat been able to demonstrate progress in talks with Israel over Palestinian autonomy on the West Bank and Gaza (as envisaged in the Camp David accords), he might have been able to prove to his Arab detractors that his methods were, after all, working. But in 1980 and 1981, Sadat's diplomacy could show little movement. The Israelis made it increasingly clear that they had no intention of giving up control of the West Bank territory which had been captured from Jordan in the 1967 War. From the standpoint of the Begin government, the West Bank was biblical Judea and Samaria and therefore part of Israel. Moreover, the Israelis believed that their own security would be jeopardized by a significant degree of Palestinian autonomy on the West Bank. To complicate matters, the Jerusalem government continued to build settlements on the West Bank and Gaza, making it plain that it had no intention of relinquishing control. The United States, like Sadat, was committed to a solution of the Palestinian problem as part of the peace process, but Washington was unwilling or unable to exert the kind of pressure on Israel that could lead to a solution. "He counted on the United States to move the peace process forward," said Eilts. When it did not, Sadat's isolation in the Arab world grew deeper.

Given his precarious position in the Arab world, it was typical of Sadat to defy his adversaries and grant asylum to the Shah of Iran. The Shah, forced from his throne by the Ayatollah Ruhollah Khomeini's Islamic revolution, had been granted brief sanctuary in Mexico, the United States and Panama; then each country, for political reasons, asked him to leave. Only in Sadat's Egypt was the promise of lifetime sanctuary freely given to a man dying and on the run. Sadat could not forget that the Shah had supplied Egypt with emergency oil during the October War, and he felt that he owed the Shah a debt of honor. A devout Muslim, he disdained the fury of Khomeini's fundamentalist supporters in Egypt and

Always a loyal friend, President Sadat risked the anger of other Arab leaders by giving asylum to the ailing former Shah of Iran when no other country would do so.

their belief in an angry God. "The relationship between man and God should not be based on fear," Sadat believed, "but on a much loftier value, the highest—friendship."

Loyalty was a supreme virtue to Sadat. After he offered refuge to the Shah, the British Foreign Secretary, Lord Carrington, asked him why he had risked certain villification in some Arab quarters. Sadat was astonished. "I don't understand you," he said. "He was my friend. Of course I will give him sanctuary." The granting of asylum to the Shah may not have been a realistic political stand, but it demonstrated courage and humanity—the hallmarks of Anwar Sadat.

For a time, Sadat's isolation from much of the Arab world did not detract from his vast prestige among the Egyptian people. Skilled in manipulating nationalist sentiments, he used the wrath of his Arab adversaries to his advantage, pointing out (with total accuracy) that some of his detractors had grown rich while Egypt had bled in four wars with Israel. In the late 1970's, Sadat enhanced his popularity when he abolished the Arab Socialist Union, the only legal political party in the country, and permitted the formation of opposition political parties. In 1979, when he was in the middle of his second six-year term as president, his National Democratic Party won over 300 seats in the 382-seat Parliament. Politically, Sadat—with the strong support of the Egyptian people and the Egyptian armed forces—dominated the country.

After the 1973 War, Sadat tried his utmost to wrench Egypt out of its age-old pattern of poverty. He turned his back on the more rigid forms of socialist economic controls and instituted an "open-door" policy designed to attract western capital, technology and consumer products. American and European companies immediately took advantage of the new liberalism, and as a result the Egyptian economy enjoyed a boom of sorts. Approximately $1 billion a year in American aid also helped, and by 1979 the country boasted a growth rate of 9 percent, the highest in the developing world.

There can be no question that the economy improved greatly under Sadat, especially considering the shambles left to him by Nasser. But if the overall economy looked fairly healthy, most Egyptians remained desperately poor, with a per capita income of just over $400 a year. When the government tried to decrease food subsidies in 1977, bloody food riots—encouraged by political extremists but based on genuine discontent—erupted in Cairo and other cities. The subsidies had to be restored.

Inflation, due in part to the rising cost of oil, was another problem; a 30 percent annual rate badly eroded the purchasing power of poorer Egyptians. Ill-clad, low-income Egyptians could only watch, smothering their anger, as their flashily-dressed, affluent countrymen spent more money in an hour in Cairo's fancy shops than they earned in years of toil.

Sadat, who never forgot his early poverty, was deeply aware of the economic gap between rich and poor. But he was genuinely convinced that a general strengthening of the economy eventually would bring widespread benefits to the common people. Sadat knew that Egypt had too many people on too little fertile land, and he nurtured visionary hopes for the future—including the reclamation of vast desert tracts for agriculture. Sadat told an American visitor: "No one can believe that America has turned, in two-hundred years, to be the most powerful, richest country in the world. I am asking my people to start like you started, the drive to the West. Everyone can achieve his ambitions. But leave this old valley (the Nile), go out and find it in the western desert! Go West, young man! And fight like fighters! Like America."

The final months of Sadat's life were not altogether happy ones. The vast majority of his countrymen supported his policies and seemed mesmerized by his personality. But negotiations with Israel had become a stormy and unproductive dialogue, giving domestic opponents the opportunity to renew their attack. The leftist National Unionist Progressive

Party publicly denounced Sadat's policy toward Israel. Said a party spokesman: "This so-called normalization of relations with Israel was done at the expense of the Arabs and is opposed by a growing number of Egyptians." In June, 1981, word spread in Cairo that the former Egyptian chief of staff, Lieut. Gen. Saad Eddin al-Shazli, and other dissidents living abroad—well supplied with money by Libya's Muammar Qaddafi—were plotting to overthrow Sadat.

MILITANT ISLAM

The major challenge to Sadat was not to come from unhappy generals or politicians capitalizing on the hardships endured by the poor. It was to come from a far different source: the fundamentalist Muslims inspired by the Islamic revolution in Iran. Early in his career as a revolutionary officer, Sadat had developed ties with the Muslim Brotherhood, a secret group of zealous fundamentalists. But those ties, which had been a matter of convenience for both Sadat and the brotherhood, eroded badly over the years. Not only the Muslim Brotherhood, but other tiny, even more fanatical offshoots looked on Sadat's western-oriented secular government as anti-Islamic.

In the late 1970's and early 1980's, Islamic associations—inspired by the rise of Khomeini in Iran—proliferated across the country. Despite Sadat's warning of "no politics in religion and no religion in politics," the associations openly advocated the total transformation of secular Egyptian society into an orthodox Islamic republic, where the stern laws of the Koran would dictate the morals and government of the country's forty-two million people. Signs of the religious revival were everywhere. Attendance at the mosques skyrocketed and reed prayer mats became a common sight in the hallways of modern office buildings at prayer times. Egyptians who occasionally sipped a glass of wine became teetotalers in accordance with Muslim practice; women who formerly wore western clothes covered their heads with scarves and their bodies with long, flowing traditional Arab gowns.

Even on the campuses, once hotbeds of western influence, the Islamic revival flourished. At most universities, the Islamic associations won control of student councils, only to have nervous school officials cancel the results on technicalities. Islamic students sparked dozens of riots in Cairo, Alexandria and other cities, resulting in deaths, injuries and thousands of arrests. The frustrated Sadat flooded the campuses with secret police and issued stern warnings to the Islamic associations, but he was unable to curb their activities or prevent the spread of their influence. In June of 1981, militants, perhaps encouraged by the Islamic associations, touched off bloody religious rioting between themselves and Coptic Christians. An estimated seventy people were killed, and the jittery Copts—who make up around seven percent of the Egyptian population—feared a revival of the nightmarish pogroms they suffered in past centuries.

In August, the fundamentalists carried their agitation right to Sadat's doorstep when a huge throng gathered outside the Abdin Palace to hail the end of Ramadan, the month-long period of fasting. The crowd ostensibly came for a prayer meeting, and some indeed held up banners proclaiming the glory of the Prophet Mohammed and quoting verses from the Koran. But a strong political undercurrent was also apparent. One banner declared: "Believers do not take the Jews and Christians as friends." Leaflets circulated through the crowd termed Sadat's peace with Israel "evil" and urged all Muslims to prepare for a *jihad*, or holy war, against Israel by eliminating the "corruption" at home.

It was all too obviously a slap at Sadat. Rumors of plots against Sadat's life by the fundamentalists began circulating. In September, he dropped his policy of tolerance and cracked down hard, jailing some 1,600 people. Most were

Muslim militants, whom he accused of stirring up trouble with the Copts; others were opposition politicians and journalists who had earned Sadat's displeasure. At the same time, mosques were "nationalized," police details were bolstered on the campuses and an investigation of anti-government activity in the bureacracy was begun. Accusing the Soviet Union of stirring up the religious dissidents, Sadat also expelled more than 1,000 Soviet civilians, including the ambassador to Egypt. Following these moves, Sadat announced that "lack of discipline in any way or form" had been ended in the country.

It was a fatal misjudgment. The cauldron of fanaticism seethed on, and from its depths were to emerge Sadat's killers. They and their accomplices were members of, or closely associated with, an offshoot of the Muslim Brotherhood known as *Takfir Wal Hijra*, a group which advocates "sacred terror." At their trial, defense lawyers entered pleas of "not guilty," but Lieut. Khaled Ahmed Shawki al-Istambuli, the leader of the murder band, could not be restrained. "I am guilty of killing Sadat and I admit that," he blurted out before the court. "I am proud of it because religion was at stake."

ANWAR SADAT'S LEGACY

8

In the days that followed Sadat's death, his enemies in the Arab world—most notably Libya's Muammar Qaddafi— called on Egyptians to rise up and overturn their government. Most Egyptians simply ridiculed such talk. Instead, they rallied around Sadat's chosen successor, Vice-President Hosni Mubarak. Sadat took great pride in having provided institutions for a peaceful transfer of power—a rare occurrence in the Arab world. The calmness and legality with which Mubarak took the helm in Cairo suggested that Sadat had done his job well.

THE OCTOBER MAN

Mubarak had been trained by Sadat for the assumption of the presidency. The two men met for the first time in the early 1950's, when Sadat was already an experienced revolutionary and Mubarak was a green, twenty-year-old officer. Even then, Sadat was impressed enough to jot down Mubarak's name in his notebook for future reference. Trained as a bomber pilot in the Soviet Union, Mubarak rose rapidly to air force chief of staff in 1969. Sadat appointed him air force commander in 1972, and a year later he led the devastating air attack on the Israeli positions that allowed the Egyptians to cross the canal on October 6. To Sadat, Mubarak was the very model of the "October man," the new kind of Egyptian capable of dealing with the Israelis and the rest of the world on equal terms. In 1975, Sadat chose Mubarak as his vice-president and political heir.

As Vice-president, the unflamboyant Mubarak was content to keep his eyes and ears open, take a low profile and leave the center of the stage to his boss. Like Sadat under Nasser's rule, Mubarak was regarded by many in Cairo as just a flunky. Many Egyptians did not know who he was, except that he was often photographed at meetings with Sadat. To some Egyptians, he was known simply as "the man who goes to meetings."

After Sadat's assassination, Mubarak made it clear that, at least for the time being, he would pursue the policies left to him by his mentor. "All I dream of now is continuing President Sadat's administration," he said. At Sadat's funeral, Mubarak met with Israeli Prime Minister Begin and the two men exchanged peace pledges. To reassure the Israeli people, Mubarak stated: "There are no changes in our policy, and I undertake to honor fully everything that President Sadat agreed to. All his commitments will be fully implemented." In other statements, Mubarak pledged total loyalty to the legacy of Sadat.

In truth, that legacy was a mixture of blessings and challenges. At home, Sadat left Mubarak a solidly established government—not totally democratic but not harshly repressive—backed by the vast majority of the Egyptian people and the armed forces. As long as Mubarak retained that backing, his presidency seemed as secure as any other leadership in the Middle East. Sadat also left behind political tensions created by his attempt, just before his death, to squelch his more outspoken opposition. More serious, perhaps, Sadat passed along to Mubarak the problem of the Islamic fundamentalists and their fanatical dream of turning Egypt into a land ruled by strict Islamic law.

Sadat bestowed on his successor an economy rich with promise but also replete with problems. The task ahead of Mubarak was to bolster the confidence of international and domestic investors, to channel that capital into solid development as well as western-style consumerism, and, most important, to make certain that the benefits of an expanding economy quickly reached the poorest Egyptians in the towns and villages.

FEAR, ENMITY AND DISTRUST

Sadat's impact on the Middle East may well prove to be a profound one. For by making peace with Israel and vowing that the two countries would never again face each other on the battlefield, he may have marked an end to the series of wars that cost both Arabs and Israelis so dearly. Most military experts agree that it would be near-suicidal for any Arab state to wage war against Israel without the support of Egypt, the strongest power in the Arab world. Still, Sadat's achievement only lessens the probability of war against Israel: it does not totally rule out the possibility. For despite his innovative genius, he could hardly fashion a total transformation of the Middle East, a region seething with fear, distrust and bitter enmity.

When Israelis contemplated the future without Sadat, the

With Vice-President
Hosni Mubarak at his side,
President Anwar Sadat
salutes a military unit
while reviewing a parade
in October 1980, one year
before his assassination.

dominant feeling was fear for the future of the peace treaty with Egypt. So thoroughly had Sadat come to personify that peace, and so deeply had Israelis come to distrust the motives of other Egyptians, that his passing swept away confidence as swiftly as his visit to Jerusalem had brought hope. Some Israelis, seeing Sadat's death as conclusive proof of the folly of signing treaties with Arab countries, launched a campaign to block the final Israeli withdrawal from the Sinai, scheduled for April, 1982. The Israeli government, however, while keeping a close eye on Mubarak and post-Sadat Egypt, vowed to keep its commitment to withdraw. As Israeli President Yitzhak Navon put it: "We did not make peace with one man, great as he was, but with the people of Egypt. We are duty-bound to continue." Other Israeli leaders took a wait-and-see attitude. "Now," said Interior Minister Yosef Burg, "we shall find out if a man or an idea was killed."

In the Arab world, Sadat's death may have brought joy to his radical and fundamentalist enemies, but it caused other leaders to begin a sober reappraisal of relations with Egypt. Sadat had annoyed some of them personally, referring to them as "dwarfs" or "lunatics" for opposing his peace with Israel. Mubarak had offended no one, and some moderate Arab states seemed ready to offer him an olive branch. Speaking for them, Chedi Klibi, secretary-general of the Arab League—which had expelled Egypt from its ranks following the signing of the peace treaty with Israel—suggested that the new Egyptian leadership renounce Camp David and "restore Egypt to its great and effective national role within the Arab family."

That poses the vexing problem Sadat left behind for Mubarak to solve: how to end Egypt's isolation among the Arabs without alarming Israel and putting an end to the peace process. Unlike his predecessor, Mubarak is a cautious man. It seemed unlikely that he would make rash moves. Eventually, however, it seemed likely that Mubarak would attempt a rapprochement with "moderate" Arab states such as Jordan and Saudi Arabia. Ideally, these countries might join Egypt in trying to find a way to a comprehensive peace in the Middle East. But those developments, if they come at all, will come slowly as Egypt tries to feel its way in the post-Sadat era.

For the United States, Egypt's course in the years ahead will be of vital importance. Both the Carter and the Reagan administrations made Sadat a key partner in the defense of western interests in the Middle East, including the security of the oil fields of the Persian Gulf. Sadat joined in that partnership wholeheartedly. He made a handshake agreement with Washington to allow the use of an air base at Ras Banas on the Red Sea as an advance staging facility for the U.S. Rapid Deployment Force, the American units that would be rushed in to deal with any trouble in the Middle East. Sadat gladly shipped arms to anti-Soviet guerrillas in Afghanistan and shared data on Libyan activities with Washington intelligence.

Some U.S. officials worried that Mubarak might attempt to loosen the close military ties that Sadat helped to forge. He is known to be unhappy at the slow pace of military deliveries from the United States. But in Washington, Mubarak was considered to be even more anti-Soviet than Sadat, and there was no fear that he would turn back to Moscow for aid and friendship. Still, having lost its best friend in the Middle East, the United States was keeping its fingers crossed.

THE LESSONS

Sadat left behind a difficult and dangerous Middle East. But in breaking the impasse of decades and daring to make peace with Israel, he may have taken—at the risk of his own life—the first crucial steps toward a full and just peace between Arabs and Israelis. In doing so, Sadat—the man who stepped to a different drummer—taught the world several lessons.

One was the tremendous importance of altering ingrained habits of thinking when old patterns of thought have proved unable to cope with reality. Without that capacity, he believed no one could hope to change reality and improve upon it. Another lesson, of first importance in a world armed to the teeth with nuclear weapons, was the absolute necessity of taking the boldest initiatives and personal risks for the cause of peace.

From time to time, Sadat had said that when the time came he hoped he would be buried in his old village of Mit Abul-Kum, among the scenes of childhood he always remembered with such delight. But in the end, it was decided that Anwar Sadat should be laid to rest in a public site near the capital. President Hosni Mubarak explained: "He was a statesman, one of the greatest in the world. How could you put him in a very small place?"

CHRONOLOGY

1918   Anwar Sadat was born on December 25 in the small village of Mit Abul-Kum.

1925   Anwar's father was transferred to Cairo, and the family moved to outskirts of the capital.

1938   Sadat graduated from the Royal Military Academy, was commissioned a second lieutenant, and was stationed in southern Egypt.

1939   Sadat transferred to Signal Corps and was stationed near Cairo.

1940   Sadat helped organize the secret Free Officers Organization, dedicated to overthrowing British rule in Egypt.

1941   Sadat engaged in clandestine anti-British activities and was arrested and interrogated, then released.

1942   Sadat arrested for his role in anti-British plot and held in the Aliens' Jail and various detention centers for next two years.

1944   Sadat escaped from jail and went into hiding.

1945   World War II ended; Sadat resumed normal life.

1946   In January, Sadat was named as a conspirator in the assassination of Amin Osman, arrested, and imprisoned for two years.

1948   From January to August, Sadat was on trial for complicity in Osman's assassination before being acquitted.

1949   Sadat married Jihan Safwat on May 29.

1950   In January, Sadat was reinstated as a captain in the Egyptian army.

1951   Sadat became influential member of Gamal Nasser's "Constituent Council" within the Free Officers Association.

1952   On the night of July 22, Nasser engineered the military coup that overthrew King Farouk; Anwar Sadat announced the revolution on Egyptian radio early in the morning of July 23.

        King Farouk went into exile on July 26.

1953   In January, the ruling revolutionary council disbanded old political parties, and assumed total governing power. The fanatical Muslim Brotherhood was outlawed.

        In March, Egypt was declared a republic. Land reform had been instituted; hospitals and schools were being built; approval was given to the idea of building a high dam at Aswan on the Nile.

1954   On October 19, the Anglo-Egyptian Evacuation Agreement was signed, providing for all British troops to leave Egypt within two years.

1955   Egypt signed first arms deal with the Soviet Union and Czechoslovakia in September.

In February, Israel raided the Gaza region of Egypt.

1956   The last British troops left their base in the Suez Canal Zone in June.

Also in June, Nasser was elected president of Egypt.

When the U.S. withdrew financing for the Aswan High Dam in July, the Soviet Union offered to build the dam.

Nasser nationalized the Suez Canal in July.

In October, Britain, France, and Israel attacked Egyptian military targets and invaded the Sinai. President Eisenhower demanded that they withdraw; the three nations complied.

1957   On January 1, Nasser nationalized all foreign businesses and financial institutions.

1958   In February, Egypt joined Syria in the ill-fated union, the United Arab Republic.

1961   The United Arab Republic was dissolved.

1965   Sadat begins privately to oppose Abdel Hakim Amer, the powerful commander in chief of the armed forces.

1967   In June, Nasser closed the Strait of Tiran, Israel's only outlet to international waters.

Israel attacked Egyptian airfields and advanced across the Sinai in the Six-Day War.

Nasser threatened to resign; Sadat persuaded him to stay on as president.

1968   In September, Nasser began the long "War of Attrition" against Israel in Sinai.

1969   Nasser named Sadat vice-president in December.

1970   Anwar Sadat became president of Egypt upon the death of Nasser in September.

On October 15, Sadat was officially elected president.

1971   During a trip to Moscow in March, Sadat rejected the arms deal offered by the Soviets.

In May, Sadat moved against his opponents, ousting pro-Soviet members of his government and ordering all tapes of private phone conversations destroyed.

1972   Sadat ordered Soviet military experts to leave Egypt by the end of July.

1973   In preparation for war against Israel, Sadat made major purchase of arms from the Soviet Union.

On October 6, Egypt staged a successful surprise attack on Israeli positions in the Sinai, beginning the October War.

Sadat accepted a cease-fire with Israel on October 19.

1974   On July 18, Secretary of State Henry Kissinger's shuttle diplomacy produced an agreement on disengagement of Egyptian and Israeli forces on the East Bank of the Suez Canal.

1975   Egypt signed a second disengagement agreement with Israel; peace process stalled.

Sadat reopened the Suez Canal for the first time since the October War.

1977   Jimmy Carter became president of the United States in January, and in May, Menachem Begin became prime minister of Israel.

On November 19, Sadat made an historic trip to Jerusalem in a bold gesture of peace toward Israel.

1978   Sadat and Begin met for thirteen days at Camp David with President Carter.

The Egyptian and Israeli leaders were awarded the Nobel Peace Prize.

1979   Sadat and Begin traveled to Washington in March

to sign the treaty that ended thirty years of confrontation between Egypt and Israel.

Sadat's efforts to attract foreign capital and technology resulted in an economic growth rate of 9 percent, the highest in the developing world.

Sadat's National Democratic Party won an overwhelming victory in parliamentary elections.

1981   In June, Egyptian dissidents abroad began to plot against Sadat.

Riots broke out between Muslim militants and Coptic Christians.

In September, Sadat cracked down on Muslim militants, opposition politicians, and journalists, and expelled 1,000 Soviet civilians, including the ambassador to Egypt.

On October 6, Anwar Sadat was assassinated by militant Muslims while reviewing a military parade commemorating the October War.

FOR FURTHER READING

Anwar Sadat's own books—*Revolt on the Nile* (New York: Day, 1957) and *In Search of Identity* (New York: Harper & Row, 1977)—are of particular interest for readers who wish to know more about his life, times and personality. Both provide fascinating insights into the mind of a unique political leader, but it should be remembered that they are highly personal accounts of the events in which Sadat took part.

A good, scholarly book on the historical background of Sadat's Egypt is *The History of Egypt from Muhammed Ali to Sadat* by P. J. Vatikiotis (Baltimore: Johns Hopkins University Press, 1980). Two readable books on the Egyptian Revolution of 1952 and the period leading up to Sadat's years in power are Robert St. John's *The Boss: The Story of Gamal Abdel Nasser* (New York: McGraw-Hill, 1960) and Jean Lacouture's *Nasser: A Biography* (New York: Alfred Knopf, 1973). An especially good, detailed evaluation of the October 1973 War is provided in military historian Edgar O'Ballance's *No Victor, No Vanquished* (San Rafael, California: Presidio Press, 1978). An excellent Israeli view of the war and its political implications for Israel is Chaim Herzog's *The War of Atonement* (Boston: Little, Brown & Co., 1975).

Other Israeli reactions to Sadat are contained in Golda Meir's *My Life* (New York: G. P. Putnam's Sons, 1975). Yitzhak Rabin's *The Rabin Memoirs* (Boston: Little, Brown & Co.,

1979) and Moshe Dayan's *Breakthrough: A Personal Account of the Egypt-Israeli Peace Negotiations* (New York: Alfred Knopf, 1981).

An acute appraisal of Sadat and his approach to making peace with Israel can be found in the second volume of Henry Kissinger's memoirs, *Years of Upheaval* (Boston: Little, Brown & Co., 1982). The former U.S. Secretary of State, an admirer of Sadat, includes illuminating anecdotes about his dealings with the Egyptian leader.

Readers are also advised to check back issues of *Newsweek, Time* and major American newspapers for the many articles on Sadat that appeared during his lifetime and at the time of his assassination.

INDEX

ABOUT THE AUTHOR

Raymond Carroll is a journalist of twenty-five years experience. As a general editor at *Newsweek*, he wrote and edited articles in the magazine's foreign affairs department, covering almost every part of the world and all aspects of foreign policy. He also served as *Newsweek's* United Nations correspondent for ten years.

Mr. Carroll is a graduate of Hamilton College and studied at Johns Hopkins University's School of Advanced International Studies. He lives in New York City where he now works as a free-lance writer.

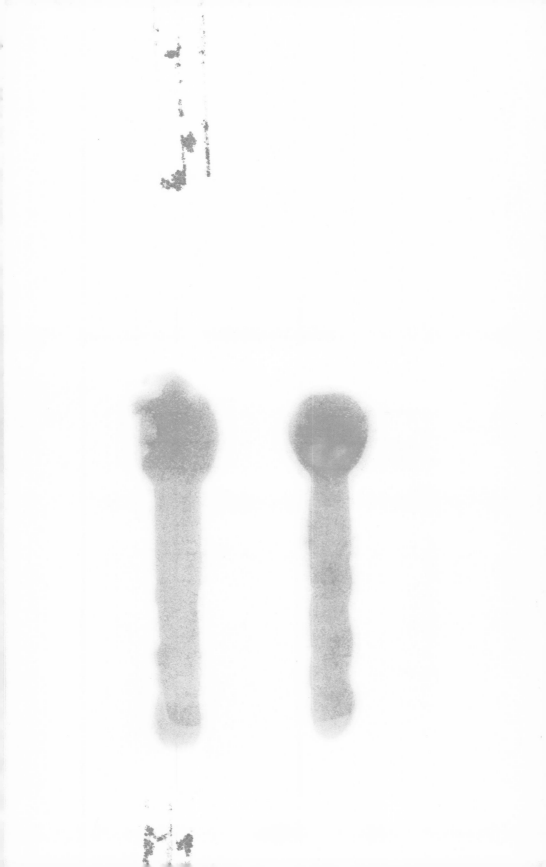

921
Sad

Carroll, Raymond

Anwar Sadat

$15.00

921
Sad

Carroll, Raymond

Anwar Sadat

St. Thomas Aquinas
High School
541 West Keith — North Vancouver